Praise for Danci

CW00740068

"Carly Abramowitz's book, must-have for navigating tc a blend of practical insights and easy-to-use tools, Carly empowers readers to embrace adaptability, foster collaboration, and drive innovation essential for success in an ever-changing environment. Through Carly's passionate and distinct perspective and creative approach, she equips readers with actionable strategies to thrive amidst complexity. This book is essential reading for anyone seeking to not only understand but actively excel in the face of constant change."

Liza Guellerin
– Global Learning Expert and Certified
Executive Coach, Louis Vuitton

"Our collaboration with Carly Abramowitz and her teams is focused on the development of essential skills to navigate a complex and uncertain world, skills that 'Dancing with Chaos' highlights perfectly. This book strongly resonates with our programs by emphasizing the importance of adaptability, relationships, and collaboration. Adaptability is essential for carrying out our audit and advisory missions; our employees are required to demonstrate continuous flexibility to remain effective with each client. This work enriches our understanding and offers new perspectives on themes that we have already integrated into our corporate culture. A valuable guide for any organization aspiring to excel in a changing environment."

Sylvaine Thomas-Penette
– Learning & Development Lead, Deloitte

"Carly Abramowitz's creativity has always been a central element of our collaboration. In 'Dancing with Chaos', she channels this energy to address the challenges of a VUCA world in a unique and relevant way. This book, with its innovative ideas and practical approaches, is a natural extension of the inventive spirit that Carly and her teams have always brought to our events. It offers fresh and stimulating perspectives, making this book a valuable resource for those looking to adapt and grow in a complex environment."

Bertrand Cheyrou
– CEO, Les Fontaines
– Serge Kampf Capgemini Campus

"As a long-standing client of Carly Abramowitz, I have implemented several training and coaching programs that closely align with the skills addressed in 'Dancing with Chaos': Confidence, Creativity, Adaptability, Collaboration. This book has perfectly encapsulated and extended the crucial principles that we have explored together. It provides an in-depth perspective on the importance of personal grounding and collective intelligence in an ever-evolving world. 'Dancing with Chaos' is an essential guide for any business looking to thrive in a dynamic environment."

Coralie Sévin
– Talent Development Manager, Ubisoft

"Our journey with the Consultative Selling programs run by CA Consulting Group led to a significant cultural shift in our business development approach. 'Dancing with Chaos' by Carly Abramowitz mirrors the changes and practices we've implemented. The book champions a client-focused and thoughtful sales methodology. It underscores the need for adaptability and understanding in a complex and quickly evolving business environment, reflecting the principles we've embraced in our corporate culture."

Frank Van Nistelrooij
– CGI Partner & VP Global Business Engineering, CGI

"Carly Abramowitz's blueprint for navigating the whirling kaleidoscope of modern life is urgent, important, and vital for anyone interested in leveraging the tidal wave of change we are caught in. It is the rare book that overlays our yearnings and fears with the often-terrifying uncertainty and aspirations of professional life. She cuts a blazing path through the uncharted territory of a shape-shifting future. Channeling hope, focus, and relationships; learning to accelerate your skills through advanced adaptability and confidence; and practicing to master a rapidly devolving business ecosystem—the rich prescriptions "Dancing in Chaos" offers are illuminating and actionable. Additionally, the book's underlying thesis—that the bewildering forces shaping our time can be harnessed to increase ingenuity, personal growth, and self-determination—provides a much-needed cathartic optimism and a case for joy."

Nusrat Durrani
– Pioneering Global Media Executive

"Carly Abramowitz, with 'Dancing with Chaos', offers a refreshing and innovative approach to the challenges of our time. Her unique style, blending creativity and applicability, makes this book particularly relevant and useful. As a reader, I was captivated by the practical teachings and adaptive strategies presented. This book is a valuable resource, offering keys to understanding and embracing the constant changes we face. It is essential for anyone wishing to remain relevant and resilient in a world of perpetual change."

Danièle Gadal
– Human Resources Director, Valéo

"Working with Carly Abramowitz for several years has revealed her unique talent for transforming soft skills into concrete practices. This ability is reflected in her book 'Dancing with Chaos'. Carly skillfully turns abstract concepts into practical and achievable tactics. This book is not just an extension of her innovative spirit, but also a practical manual for those looking to acquire fundamental skills in a rapidly changing world. Her approach, which blends theory with practical application, makes this work indispensable."

Franck Baillet
– Executive Vice President - Learning &
Development France, Capgemini

"In our context of rapid and highly impactful transformations, Carly Abramowitz and her teams have been able to support our management and high potentials in the development of their leadership and adaptability. Her work 'Dancing with Chaos' offers a pragmatic approach that allows leaders to evolve in the uncertainty of a VUCA world. Carly consistently conveys the core of these teachings in her keynote speeches, adeptly engaging her audience with this profound realization."

Carine Noémie
– Head of Professional Development &
Coach, AG2R La Mondiale

"In a world where technology plays a dominating role in our life, *Dancing with Chaos* is a necessary refocuser back to all the essential soft skills that make us human. This book is for anyone looking to not just survive this period of AI and automation but thrive within it."

Evan Ryan
– Founder Teammate AI

"Carly is a master of simplifying the complex. With a deep compassion for people, and a unique talent for training and coaching. In 'Dancing with Chaos,' Carly masterfully captures the essence and beauty of navigating our ever-changing landscape with grace and adaptability. This book not only aligns with the core principles we champion at AQai but contextualizes and elevates them, offering a practical roadmap to harnessing adaptability in the face of complexity. Carly is an esteemed AQ Certified Partner, who explores the symbiotic relationship between adaptability and thriving amidst chaos. Her three-step approach empowers readers to move toward their goals with renewed purpose and confidence. 'Dancing with Chaos' is a catalyst for transformation, inspiring action and equipping you with the tools to live your best life in an exponential world. A must-read for anyone looking to embrace change and turn challenges into opportunities."

Ross Thornley
– Serial Entrepreneur,
Author, and Co-Founder of AQai.

"In her book 'Dancing with Chaos', Carly Abramowitz shares practical strategies that reflect her expertise in managerial skill development. Her approach, focused on emotional intelligence and behavioral skills, is highly effective. Thanks to her guidance, our managers have become more at ease and impactful in their communications. They are even more committed to developing the potential of their teams and lead their activities with increased clarity and efficiency. Her vision of leadership is a source of inspiration and a practical guide for any manager seeking improvement."

Antoine Valverde
– Head of CAP Compétences Corporate University,
Crédit Mutuel Alliance Fédérale

"Digital natives are used to saying that Digital is like a jungle. If you don't run when the sun rises someone will eat you. Your competitor, your colleagues, the market, your clients or just another trend. *Dancing with Chaos* is a great book and manual for waking up and taking the steps to move with the change. In the fast-paced world of digital marketing and social media, *Dancing with Chaos* by Carly Abramowitz, emerges as a critical read for anyone looking to understand and leverage the power of change in the digital landscape and to adopt techniques that that can make you tick.

As the Founder and CEO of Blink Havas a digital first agency, I've seen firsthand how adaptability and creativity are key to crafting compelling brand strategies that resonate in today's market. Abramowitz's insights into navigating chaos with agility and foresight are invaluable for marketing professionals seeking to stay ahead of the curve. This book is a must-have for those committed to leading their brands to new heights in an ever-evolving digital environment."

Sagi Chemetz
– Founder & CEO Blink Havas

"Carly Abramowitz's 'Dancing with Chaos' is a vital read for today's dynamic business environment. As a training expert in the sciences of understanding people, I found the book's focus on resilience, communication, and relationship building insightful. This book is an essential guide for anyone seeking to excel in both their personal and professional lives, offering practical strategies and actions for developing the comprehensive skills needed in today's competitive and challenging landscape."

Krista Sheets
– President, Competitive Edge, Inc.

"Having benefited from the coaching programs of CA Consulting Group for our employees over the years, 'Dancing with Chaos' by Carly Abramowitz perfectly reflects our various experiences. This work gives wings to wounded birds and then pushes the flock to fly more effectively together, with unity and cooperation. It offers a new approach and practical strategies that enrich and strengthen leadership and collaboration. This book is a treasure for those looking to deepen their understanding and application of key skills in a changing world."

Valérie Rome
– Head of Training, Assurances Crédit Mutuel

"Carly Abramowitz's 'Dancing with Chaos' is an enlightening journey through the complexities of our era, offering a compelling argument for the role of creativity and innovation in forging paths through uncertainty. This book aligns with the notion that breakthroughs often come from the least expected scenarios, challenging us to rethink our approach to problem-solving. Abramowitz provides not just a set of tools but a mindset shift essential for anyone committed to making a difference in an ever-evolving world."

Abdallah Hitti
– Serial Entrepreneur & Managing Partner Eurofed
France & Brapago Global CrossBorder Payment Leader

DANCING
WITH
CHAOS

THREE STEPS TO BREAK FREE FROM COMPLEXITY, MOVE TOWARD YOUR GOALS FASTER, AND LIVE YOUR BEST LIFE

DANCING
WITH
CHAOS

**THREE STEPS TO BREAK FREE FROM COMPLEXITY,
MOVE TOWARD YOUR GOALS FASTER,
AND LIVE YOUR BEST LIFE**

CARLY ABRAMOWITZ

ethos
collective

DANCING WITH CHAOS © 2024 by Carly Abramowitz.
All rights reserved.

Printed in the United States of America

Published by Ethos Collective™
PO Box 43, Powell, OH 43065
www.ethoscollective.vip

This book contains material protected under international and federal
copyright laws and treaties. Any unauthorized reprint or use of this
material is prohibited. No part of this book may be reproduced or trans-
mitted in any form or by any means, electronic or mechanical, including
photocopying, recording, or by any information storage and retrieval
system, without express written permission from the author.

LCCN: 2023923822
Paperback ISBN: 978-1-63680-256-5
Hardcover ISBN: 978-1-63680-257-2
e-book ISBN: 978-1-63680-258-9

Available in paperback, hardcover, e-book, and audiobook.

Any Internet addresses (websites, blogs, etc.) and telephone numbers
printed in this book are offered as a resource. They are not intended in
any way to be or imply an endorsement by Ethos Collective™, nor does
Ethos Collective™ vouch for the content of these sites and numbers for
the life of this book.

Some names and identifying details may have been changed to protect
the privacy of individuals.

Table of Contents

Part One: The Basics of Dance Being Rooted

Part Two: Discovering Acceleration Skills

Part Three: Navigational Skills

Part Four: Let Yourself Dance

Foreword by Dan Sullivan

In an era marked by rapid technological advances and societal shifts, *Dancing with Chaos* offers a profound roadmap for thriving amidst the agitation. This book resonates with the core teachings at Strategic Coach®, where we encourage embracing change as an opportunity for growth and innovation.

As someone who has dedicated his life to coaching entrepreneurs to achieve greater freedom and results, I see Carly Abramowitz's work as a vital playbook for anyone looking to gracefully navigate the complexities of our modern era. Carly provides a compass for us all, illuminating how to move with agility and purpose in an ever-changing landscape.

This is not a book that dwells on the challenges of our times. It's a story that celebrates the potential within each of us to navigate these challenges with grace and strength.

Carly's insights inspire us to view the complexities of our world not as barriers, but as the very elements that can propel us to new heights of achievement and fulfillment.

Throughout this insightful narrative, Carly adeptly translates the principles of entrepreneurial thinking into a broader context. She addresses not only leaders but anyone who faces the daily dance of managing personal and professional challenges in a rapidly evolving environment. It's about understanding the rhythm of change and learning how to move in sync with it, rather than being overwhelmed by its pace.

Carly's concept of Edge Skills™ is particularly relevant. These skills – adaptability, emotional intelligence, resilience – are crucial not just in leadership but in every aspect of our lives. They are the tools that enable us to pivot gracefully in response to unforeseen obstacles and seize opportunities that arise in a world where the only constant is change.

As we get into *Dancing with Chaos*, we find ourselves not just reading, but engaging in a conversation about transformation. Carly encourages us to embrace the fluidity of our times, to find our unique rhythm in the cacophony of the digital age. This book is a testament to the power of a growth mindset, a theme we emphasize at Strategic Coach, where the goal is not just to survive but to thrive amid change.

In Carly's world, dancing with chaos doesn't mean getting lost in the turmoil; it means finding your path, your pace, and your purpose. It's about turning the unpredictable nature of our world into a dance floor where every step, no matter how tricky and uncertain, leads to growth and discovery. It's about leveraging the chaos not as an adversary but as a partner in our pursuit of progress and purpose.

So, as you turn the pages of *Dancing with Chaos*, prepare to embark on a journey of self-discovery and empowerment. Carly Abramowitz invites you to join the dance through the music of your own unique journey. Embrace the tempo, feel the rhythm, and prepare to take the stage with confidence. The spotlight is on, the music has started, and it's time to dance.

—Dan Sullivan
Co-Founder & President of Strategic Coach®

Use Genie™ to Get the Most Out of This Book

"Dancing with Chaos" dives deep into 18 essential skills crucial for thriving in today's rapidly changing world. In an era where AI is a main driver of exponential change, it's vital we learn to dance with it.

Each chapter focuses on a specific skill—from adaptability and creativity to collaboration and resilience. These are actionable strategies for daily life to stay ahead in this dynamic environment.

As AI revolutionizes routine tasks, it opens the door for people to focus on creativity, collaboration, and emotional intelligence, making these soft skills more essential than ever. AI can be your powerful ally in developing these skills.

That's why I'm thrilled to introduce you to Genie™, your personal AI companion for "Dancing with Chaos". Genie™ is your personal growth partner.

At the end of each skill chapter, you'll find a Practical Tips section with special prompts for Genie™, guiding you through tailored exercises. Additionally, there are three manual exercises to further develop each skill.

Embrace the journey, engage deeply with the exercises, and let Genie™ guide you as you learn to dance with chaos and thrive in the ever-evolving world.

You can connect with Genie™ on www.talk2genie.com or using the QR Code below.

Introduction

Learning to Dance

Two people moving in harmony to a subtle beat mesmerizes audiences. Each time we add a person to the synchronization, the performance becomes even more awe-inspiring, and when a few of those dancers move out of sync, creating their own motion and beauty yet somehow keeping tempo with the company, we watch in amazement.

While everyone can dance, only those willing to put their entire soul into the art can feel the rhythm and create the flow that makes people want to watch. But what gives these artists the ability to bring the music to life? How can they turn an auditory experience into a visual display of energy and emotion?

In 2011, I read an article by Ray Kurzweil predicting a merge of man and machine by 2045. He hypothesized that artificial intelligence would advance to the point that it will be able to read brain wavelengths and decipher a human's motivations and truthfulness. I suppose as computers learn the many aspects of dance they may one day be able to keep us as engaged as the real thing, but at the time, as a communications specialist, I wondered if AI would one day replace me as a corporate negotiation coach.

You might think that dialectic methods are very twenty-first century, but people have been using these advanced negotiation techniques in hostile environments since the ancient Greeks developed them to protect democracy. However, our team employed dialectic practices to help our client, a cosmetics giant, ensure a truthful debate as they negotiated. Using creative and confrontational strategies, we can weed out untruthful influencers and find peaceful solutions.

It was aboard that plane to my client's training center that I read Kurzwiel's article. His ideas intrigued me so much that I signed up for his program—Singularity University. I got to see the advances of artificial intelligence and robotics technology up close. One woman who had been paralyzed fifteen years prior in a skiing accident was able to stand and hug her mother courtesy of exoskeletal technology. It was exciting to see things designed for military initiatives bring quality to someone's life.

Though the program lasted only one week, it left me forever changed. I encountered seventy-nine individuals who shared my abundance mindset. We believed we could change the world. The energy in the room as well as the positive-mindsets and the potential to use technology to create exponential growth reinforced my ideals on the importance of positive-minded community.

I returned to Paris excited about the possibilities beginning to open up thanks to technology. Not everyone shared my enthusiasm. Some thought perhaps I'd been brainwashed, and others saw only negativity and the potential for evil with the advancements in AI.

Of course, everything can be used for evil, but developing a prosperity mindset let me see the good that could come if humanity positioned the smartest tech people in the world to focus on ethical programming and design. I have a genie-in-the-bottle philosophy. Once the genie has been released—or technology, in this case—we can't put it back in, we can only work toward shaping it as positively as possible.

Linear Versus Exponential Growth

Singularity's teaching stems from an understanding of linear versus exponential growth. Linear growth deals with a very anticipated and constant rate of change. In math, linear patterns involve addition—2+3=5+3=8+3=11. Exponential growth deals in multiplication. So, even when the rate is constant, the growth is much faster—2x3=6x3=18x3=54. As you can see in those two examples, in just three steps exponential growth takes us forty-three paces further than linear growth, and if the growth occurs in tens rather than threes, the spread increases by almost two thousand.

Since the dawn of civilization, humanity has been learning, creating, and improving. However, until early in the twenty-first century that growth remained very linear. In 1900, knowledge doubled about every one hundred years. By the end of 1945, the doubling rate increased to once every twenty-five years. In 2010, Eric Schmidt, the CEO of Google, reported that every two days humans were creating the same amount of data they did in all the years prior to 2003.[1] Eric

Schmidt and Ray Kurzweil now estimate the "Knowledge Doubling Curve" has reached the twelve-hour mark. [2]

The Consequences of Linear Thinking in a World of Exponential Growth

In the midst of all this growth, the human mind remains very linear. We think in terms of hours and months. When developing a five-year plan, we have a difficult time wrapping our brain around the exponential growth we need to account for.

Additionally, despite the exponential growth of technology and information, social, political, and many business structures continue to progress in a linear motion. For example, just a few years after I attended Singularity, several of my biggest projects were canceled. We'd prepared huge change-management curriculums for Human Resources Departments to roll out with thousands of managers and leaders in their companies, and after months of preparation for each project, all three were canceled at the last minute.

The first two cancellations bothered me, and I blamed them on a bad year. But by the time the third one called, I knew I needed to find out what was going on.

Much of the chaos actually dated back to the consequences of the 2008 financial crisis. Companies started reframing their strategies on a more frequent basis following that difficult time. The time frames got smaller and smaller until employees became exhausted as they constantly had to learn new techniques and processes and adapt to new plans and goals.

My company got caught in the crossfire as my clients' visions and strategies went through that kind of massive reconstruction. Their pivot in thinking, along with the exponential information curve, meant the leadership of the companies changed their strategies enough in just six months that the training we'd planned became irrelevant.

They apologized for the cancellation and appreciated my hard work, but they felt a need to regroup. By the time they had implemented the current strategies, a shift in leadership would bring new ideas and strategies. And with them came an entirely new kind of chaos.

Running from the Chaos or Dancing with It

Such fast-paced consistent change brings extreme discomfort. It's the equivalent of an orchestra warming up—every instrument playing a different scale or motif—with no end in sight. The lack of rhythm and predictable melody leave the dancers feeling tension, and the constant barrage of indistinguishable notes sounds like mayhem rules. The changing culture feels just as confusing and noisy.

Most people run from that kind of never-ending confusion. Unplanned change feels dangerous. Many worry the extended upheaval will steal their job. But the change created to combat the confusion just causes more upheaval. Fear and stress set in. Technology becomes the enemy because, let's face it, what will we do if a robot can do our job?

As grocers all over the world installed self-checkouts, entire layouts of the stores changed, employees needed new training, and customers were forced to adjust. Linear brains rejected the advancement because it looked like a huge mess. Few saw the value of the machines when they saw a single human left to help the elderly, handicapped, and pregnant with their check-out.

Though the technology has been around for more than a decade, society has been resistant to adapt. It causes chaos as we train cashiers and waitresses to coach customers through the self-checkouts and pay-at-the-table apps. Mayhem arises when familiar stores and restaurants rearrange their floorplan to accommodate the technology.

As the exponential growth of technology outpaces the linear thinking of the mind, the world becomes uncomfortable. Things we've grown to expect and enjoy transform, and for most, it's unpleasant. We have a choice—run from the chaos or dance with it.

My experience at Singularity helped me understand the exponential technology curve; however, the turbulence created by the exponential growth of the information age didn't really hit my company until 2015.

For the next three years, people ran from the chaos. It became increasingly difficult to plan training for clients, so we revised our curriculum to teach managers how to handle a series of successive changes rather than just a single management change. Our programs became focused on how to manage within a constant climate of revisions. It took several years of slow, incremental growth for us to climb out of the disturbance caused by the collision of linear thinking with the Knowledge Doubling Curve. But clients finally came to see the value of teaching leaders and collaborators to acquire high-level adaptability and change management skill-sets by 2021.

Becoming Client-Centric in the Chaos

The chaos of the exponential brought a pressure I'd never seen before. Entrepreneurial life can be overwhelming, but by 2018 it felt out of control. Like most small business owners, I usually do a million things at one time. I thought part of the encumbrance came from the lifestyle I had created. Then I noticed that even my clients who were employees inside large corporations were feeling the same strain.

I commute between Miami and Paris throughout the year. And while my American schedule remains constant, the French calendar offers stretches of calm downtime. However, that year everyone I talked to complained about the never-ending to-do list, and not just during the usually intense months of June, October, and November. The restful French summer and holidays had become chaotic. Even employees of the highly protected French social system felt the burden.

Singularity had predicted that the pace of change would continue to accelerate; however, without preparing for the acceleration, everyone's schedule felt the impact. Technology was supposed to improve the quality of our life and free us from many of our tasks. How could we manage this exponential chaos curve that accompanied the acceleration of the information age?

I quickly noticed that those companies weathering the storm of information had become client-centric. Relationship focused businesses set themselves apart from their competitors. So, my company began to look for creative ways for our clients' sales and delivery teams to connect in a more authentic way with their own clients.

Though a number of people since 1930 have been credited with coining the phrase Emotional Intelligence, the practical applications of the non-tech ability weren't mined until the 1990's. Today, Harvard Business School calls it the "key to professional success." [3]

Today our sales training puts great emphasis on creating a deep relationship with the client because this human factor makes all the difference. In this ever-changing fast-paced climate, the personal connection and individual attention set companies apart from their competition.

The Knowledge Curve Raises the Need for Community

Since my days of studying and performing in the theater, I've seen the power of relationship and community. My experience with Singularity reinforced this idea. Spending that week with like-minded individuals brought energy to the room, an energy that stayed with me for months. In my own life, I have many arenas for community, and I value each one. I find six most prominent in my life right now.

- My family, including my children and parents.

- My team at CA Consulting Group

- My summer camp "family" from my childhood—a place my son now attends.

- My theater friends from Northwestern University and my former life as an actress.

- The Abundance360 community which brings 360 entrepreneurs together annually to solve the world's greatest challenges.

- The Strategic Coach® community, a group of successful entrepreneurs that bond through a concept developed by Dan Sullivan called The Four Freedoms®: Time, Relationships, Money, and Purpose.

These communities provide love, support, encouragement, inspiration, and guidance, plus they challenge me to always be my best self. I see growth in my life because of these individuals. They increase my drive, confidence, ambition, motivation, and determination.

Society has become less spiritual and more secular over the past one hundred years. Technology has given us hundreds and perhaps even thousands of connections never before possible, yet people feel more alone now than ever. [4] In order to thrive in the chaos, we need to learn to dance.

Dancing has many advantages. The movement improves our cardiovascular system, gives us more flexibility, and builds our core strength. It's good for our bones, weight loss, and memory. But more importantly, it can help us deal with the chaos. Research shows that dance decreases anxiety, increases self-esteem, busts our stress, and keeps us from feeling lonely or socially isolated. [5]

Dance allows us to connect in a way few other activities do. We learn to become synchronous and independent at the same time. Each dancer follows the same rhythm, and while sometimes the movements mimic or mirror, at other times, they push and pull. Learning intricate footwork and the nuances of the people you dance with make the visual even more beautiful. And the music occasionally adds minors or power chords that add tension and suspense to the art.

The dance of life looks much the same. Life sometimes seems confusing and disconnected, but at the same time, we need each other. We come together, connect, and align. The tension between the exponential knowledge curve and linear thinking is like those suspenseful musical motifs, beautiful and adventurous if we embrace the movement.

When I moved recently, one of the movers on the team I hired thought I might be concerned because they didn't talk much as they lifted furniture and moved about the apartment. He explained that they'd been working together so long they knew what the others' next steps would be without saying a word. They had learned the dance of their profession.

Every highly skilled team can reach that level of attunement. I had a similar connection with my fellow actors at Northwestern. When I learned to let go of the chatter in my own head, I instinctively knew the next movements of everyone else on stage. That's connection in action.

Developing a Skill Set Rooted in Purpose

Technology will never be able to replace the human connection. That's why relationships have become one of the most vital elements in the success of business. Companies can move in complete rhythm with the exponential curve of technology, but without finding the music that speaks to their clients and connecting and aligning with them, the potential for beauty will be lost.

As our team maneuvered through the effects of the exponential acceleration of knowledge, we discovered a skill set that helped my company address the tension caused by the massive speed of technological advances interacting with the linear mind. We discovered that leaders needed to be trained to be change managers.

By focusing on emotional intelligence and helping leaders and their teams better understand people skills, we can help corporations move the dial toward enhanced performance and well-being while managing the transformation required to keep up with the ever-increasing curve.

Before we can apply the skill set you'll find in the following pages, we have to define our purpose. I divide the skills into three sets: Rooting Skills, Acceleration Skills, and Navigational Skills. But these important traits need a foundation; they need purpose. Most business strategists call it your "Why."

Your purpose gives you a clear sense of center. Your "Why" underpins your hope and enthusiasm and lets your inner light shine. It will drive your acceleration skills and provide the reference point for your navigational skills, and all of it is rooted in hope, courage, focus, strong relationships, creativity, and practice.

Even if you know your purpose, it's critical to continually refine it. As you grow and change, your purpose will morph and expand.

Every year at Abundance360, Peter Diamandis invites us to rewrite our Massive Transformative Purpose (MTP). By connecting to and upgrading our purpose annually, we can enter the next twelve months with fresh clarity. Likewise, during our Strategic Coach sessions, Dan Sullivan continually reminds us to make sure our future is bigger than our past.

One of my company's programs provides a methodology for discovering and refining your purpose. We ask questions that point you toward your purpose:

- Why is your focus important to you?

- Why is it important to others?

- Who do you serve?

- How are you contributing and giving back to the world?

- What inspires and motivates you?

My company's purpose is "Empowering people to thrive in a transforming world." So, we ask, "Why is that important to our team?"

I deeply admire organizations like Doctors Without Borders—men and women willing to go into dangerous parts of the world to save lives and carry out their mission. Your purpose doesn't have to be as life threatening as those doctors to have as much value. Your commitment and motivation give your purpose meaning.

As you grow and evolve, your purpose may radically change. It takes courage to make those changes, but it's vital to live out your passion if you want to practice the skills I'm about to share.

Throughout history, chaos has revealed the potential in humanity. Imagine the mayhem in transporting goods before someone came up with the wheel. And sharing information had obviously caused chaos for years before Gutenberg mechanized printing after countless great minds had come up with solutions that inspired the German inventor. Danger and lost life inspired someone in the Han Dynasty to produce a compass, and what kind of chaos would rule without the many means of communication we have today?

Many try to avoid the confusion and instability caused by the digital age. They live in a world of fear and scarcity. Imagine what the world must look like to those who've reached their hundredth birthday. They never imagined the four-inch screens they watched when televisions were introduced would someday have hundreds of options for viewing. Likewise, we can't imagine the exponential developments that will occur in our lifetime. Some will run from the change, but those who learn to embrace the disturbance will thrive. Will you bury your head in the sand and be a prophet of doom, or will you see the possibility, live in the excitement of the potential, and start dancing with the chaos?

PART ONE

The Basics of Dance
Being Rooted

When a ballerina begins her lessons, she'll learn the five arm and feet positions and how to transition between them. The instructor may give the class a count, but the music won't start until the class has a good foundation. Ballroom dancers learn postures and steps as well as the different kinds of dances before they take their art to the public.

A dancer's purpose is to dance, but they can't carry out their purpose until they've learned the fundamentals. Likewise, in this fast-paced world, we need some basic skills to root us and keep us steady when the chaos tries to get us off beat.

The linear rooting of the early twentieth century—marriage, home-ownership, children, and entering a lifetime career—doesn't fit the chaos of the exponentially expanding twenty-first century. Rather than traditional milestones and external influences that can change as fast as the information we download, humans need an internal rooting, one that shapes how we view the world and is molded by those we surround ourselves with. With the right rooting skills, we can move through this wobbly world with confidence and learn the basic steps that will help us dance with the chaos.

1

Hope

A young man and his father were struggling in business. The son wanted to give up and close up shop, but the father wanted to keep going. The son didn't understand what motivated his father. To explain, the older man took the younger out to a large well. Though the son couldn't swim, his father asked him to jump in. Finally, the father pushed his son into the well and went into hiding. For five minutes, the young man tried to keep his head above water, but since he couldn't swim, he finally gave up. Just as he took in a gulp of water instead of air, his father came to his rescue.

The next day, they repeated the scenario, but this time the father disappeared for fifteen minutes. When he returned, his son was struggling desperately, but keeping his head above water just fine. As the older man pulled the younger from the water, he asked, "What was different today that you were able to keep from drowning for so long." The son answered, "I had hope. I knew you would come and save me before I drowned." [6] That's what hope can do. It helps us hold on when it looks like the chaos is about to take us under. Hope begins internally as a little light in the darkness.

It's easy to let our failures and unfulfilled dreams steal our joy. Hope has a vision and faith in the future. It provides energy to push us forward in the face of the unknown.

When Hope Wanes

About the time I turned thirty, I felt a bit lost. I had expected to be an actress and a writer by then. I coached to make a living, but the vision I had for my life wasn't panning out. Around the same time period, my parents divorced, and family relationships were tense. Everything in my life seemed out of sync, hard, and disappointing.

People around me began to move forward in their lives, but I couldn't hear the music. Even after I started CA Consulting Group to sustain me financially and pursue my dream, insecurity loomed. Feeling like a failure, hope became a fleeting thing.

People lose hope for a number of reasons. For starters, hope as well as the lack of hope are contagious. Like a case of smallpox, if everyone around us begins to catch the disease of negativity in their struggles, there's a good chance we'll catch it too. This disease grows in the face of financial, emotional, and psychological suffering or physical danger. Father Greg, priest in the poorest Catholic parish in Los Angeles, said, "Gang violence is the lethal absence of hope." [7]

Mindset Training

To pull myself out of hopelessness, I started listening to subliminal, affirmative recordings. By reconditioning my way of thinking, I believed I could regain myself. I listened every night before I fell asleep, and while it took some time, my perspective started to change, and I felt a restored sense of hope giving me energy to go forward.

A big part of learning to have hope is found in changing our perspective. In this world of exponential technological advances, we expect faster wi-fi and better living conditions. We feel cheated if someone else gets the contract, and when we find ourselves encumbered by someone else's shortcomings, we feel frustration. It's easy to get caught in the entitlement trap, a dreary place void of beauty. Entitlement mindset focuses on what we should have. Envy feeds it as we see what others have worked for and wonder why we've been left out.

I never met my great-grandfather, but my grandmother told me stories about him. They came to the United States in 1938, essentially at the last moment before the borders fully closed during the Holocaust. A fairly wealthy Jewish-German family, my great-grandfather had a successful business and a beautiful house with housekeepers and cooks. My grandmother told me about their luxurious vacations and upper-class lifestyle.

However, when my great-grandparents left Germany, they also left behind all that wealth and comfort. They weren't allowed to take anything with them.

My great-grandfather was in his late fifties when he began working at Yale as a cafeteria cook. My grandmother said her father remained a happy man because he chose to always look down rather than look up. He believed that when you look down, you can see people who have been dealt a worse hand than you, filling you with gratitude for what you have. Looking up reveals the people you think have more than you or fared better, and you feel bitter or deprived. My great-grandfather could have dwelt on his good life in Germany. Instead, he focused on the fact his family was alive. Everything else was secondary.

When my first child was born, I hired a nanny from the Philippines. She'd come to France so she could send money back to help her family. After a few months, I learned that during her first year in Paris, she'd been raped, had a child, and taken that baby back to the Philippines for her family to raise. She hadn't seen her daughter for five years.

Meanwhile, I'd been nitpicking about how to put the dishes away and which pajamas James should wear. Her story and her positive attitude despite her circumstances helped me reign in my entitlement attitude. I began to see things from her perspective, and, like my great-grandfather, I started to appreciate my life more.

A young mother in Miami helped shape my mindset as well. The youngest of her four children had been shot in Columbia when he was two. In a completely separate incident, she'd lost her husband in a similar manner.

Both of these women's stories shaped my life forever. I learned to take projects less seriously and rethink the things that caused me irritation and frustration. When we feel entitled to something without struggle, it's difficult to tap into hope for something better.

Hope pulls us out of bad situations. Watch videos of children in war-torn countries when relief organizations visit. These young people who live in the worst of conditions dance and laugh because volunteers delivered more than just food and medical supplies—they delivered hope.

My Miami friend runs an association for underprivileged children in Columbia. I admire her ability to steward the project from so many miles away, and she inspires me to help whenever I can. She has a passion for those Columbian children, and her efforts provide hope in her home country.

Hope is available to everyone regardless of where you're from or what your role is—from the laborer to the CEO of a Fortune 500 company. One of my Parisian friends kept hope through the ten years he and his wife had to be away from their children. From toddlers to teens, they missed a huge portion of their children's lives, yet the couple never gave up believing they would be able to bring their children to Paris one day.

Hope is not dependent on circumstances; it's centered on your mindset. You have the power to change your perspective by learning to focus on the positive rather than the negative. A big part of changing our mindset comes when we change our community.

Community Building

A huge shift in my mindset came when I began to build a more supportive and positive-minded community. During the time I started listening to the motivational and positive recordings, I also invested in Jay Abraham's School of Marketing, coaching with John Asaraff, and personal development with Joe Vitale. Despite my meager finances at the time, I found a way to pay for these programs. Each gave me a hope-based community with a positive outlook, and their intrinsic value far outweighed their cost. The experience became a two-way energy circuit that built shared hope.

The communities that I mentioned in the introduction each provide hope in a unique and positive way. Family, friends, and co-workers each pour positivity into my life. Like the young man whose father rescued him, I know these people who are in my life daily will jump in and pull me out on those days when hope is hard to find.

The crowd at Strategic Coach and Abundance360 boost my hope every time we meet. They fill the room with light and energy that I take back and pass along to those communities at home.

No one is immune to those feelings of hopelessness. In fact, everyone faces them at some point in their life. However, plugging into a system that fosters hope helped me stay on track.

Consider the art of dance. Yes, solo dancing is beautiful; however, on those days when hope wanes, it's challenging to dance alone. When we feel tired, frustrated, or hopeless, having a dance partner helps us hear the music and stay in rhythm. Sometimes the partner literally lifts the ballerina in the middle of the dance, and often we need the same kind of support. How can that happen if we don't have a strong community full of hope?

Hope in Business

Farmers offer one of the best illustrations of hope in business. Seeds planted in the spring take weeks to sprout and months to produce. They depend on the weather as well as the soil conditions. Most people don't realize how much can go wrong in the field. In fact, it's so risky, some who farm for a living purchase crop insurance as a backup. Still, despite the knowledge that the rain may not cooperate, hail might wipe out the entire field, or deer could eat the full crop just before it's ready to harvest, those men and women have hope that when they plant those seeds, most of them will bring a harvest.

Every avenue of business and life offers similar risks and abundance. You make the effort to lay the groundwork for success, but problems arise and performance wanes. When

I face difficulties in my business, I remind myself that I'm planting seeds, and it will take time to see results.

Entrepreneurs face many hard days, weeks, quarters, and years. Anyone who runs a business knows what I'm talking about. I called a professional colleague recently. When I asked him how he was, he said, "I'm having an entrepreneur day." It was one of those days—he didn't get the project, couldn't start his big idea, his amazing new hire decided to quit, or another of the pitfalls of entrepreneurial life struck.

Hope gets us through those rough patches and bolsters our leadership abilities. Additionally, because hope is contagious, our hope brings hope to others. As a business owner or leader in your industry, it's important to examine the hope you bring to others and how it unifies and motivates them. There have been many junctures in my career when I wouldn't have had the grit to keep going had I lacked a larger, hopeful vision.

Entrepreneurship is itself a tremendous act of hope. Less than seventy percent of businesses survive two years, and fewer than that celebrate their tenth anniversary. [8]

Whether you're an entrepreneur, an employee, or a parent, hope is key. Some of my friends are managing difficult issues with their adolescent or older children. They need hope to stay the course during tough developmental times; otherwise, they'll become fixated on the negative and potentially damage the relationship.

My company has weathered a host of salespeople over the years. When I couldn't seem to find the right candidate, I had to keep at it, because I believe in the service we offer and our vision. I wanted my company to grow and succeed. Working on a project requires managing the setbacks.

You'll need a variety of skills to accelerate and navigate the complexities of the business world but hope underlies them all. There's a time for planting, growing, and harvesting.

Seeing the process through requires faith that what you're planting will eventually yield a harvest. It also requires acceptance that sometimes what you plant doesn't grow in the way you expected, or at all. In those cases, you need the vision, energy, and desire that spring from hope to motivate you to plant again.

The World Needs Hope-filled Leaders

Dance teachers with the greatest influence lead with a spirit of hope. They bring positivity to their students' lives and help them see their mistakes as room for improvement rather than failures. Allowing people to see the potential of what can be fosters hope, and it's an essential skill for leaders.

Hope possesses a binding and unifying force that brings people together and helps them overcome life's difficulties. As a result, they can do amazing things together.

Those who let their inner light of hope shine set themselves apart. Even if you aren't in a leadership position yet, if you can communicate a positive vision and inspire others to forge ahead when times are difficult, you can be a leader in any ecosystem. Every move builds the future. We can build with a negative, pessimistic vision or a hopeful one. You choose the seeds you plant. What do you prefer to see in your garden—thistles or sunflowers?

Leaders have the added responsibility of monitoring and feeding their hope. They set the tone for a positive or negative future. We all leave an impact, but leaders have greater influence. When leaders communicate a clear, positive, hopeful vision—whether in the short term, long term, or somewhere between—they take responsibility for that influence and their role in shaping the future. We don't need perfection or pasted smiles, but we do need leaders who are aware of the power they wield.

What energy do you share with people? Do you communicate abundance or scarcity? Do you accept responsibility for the impact you have on others? The vision, energy, and ideas you put into the world make a difference. As a leader, stay conscious of the fact that people look to you for guidance and to set the tone.

Leadership can be a lonely place. In 2016, I participated in a team coaching program led by Ruth Wageman, a Harvard researcher. She has done brilliant work on team dynamics and what she calls "leader attribution error." She points out how easy it is to pin mistakes, problems, or setbacks on the leader simply because they're in charge. As a result, leaders risk becoming defensive and isolated.

The communities we discussed earlier can be a great solution to combating solitude. We cultivate our hope and positivity through support systems. They allow us to see our role more clearly so that we can take responsibility for our mistakes as well as our achievements. These positive communities give us the space to see the positive when the blame for everything wrong lands on our shoulders. These energy-filled people restore our vision so we can be a source of hope and a positive example.

True leaders offer a beacon of hope when the world seems dark and desolate. When we model hope in the midst of chaos, we help others get into the right mindset. Hope flows when you are for something rather than against the alternative. Hope-filled leaders promote the positive rather than fixate on the negative. George Washington wasn't anti-England; he was pro-freedom. Martin Luther King Jr. wasn't anti-violence; he was pro-peace. A positive vision offers a concrete place for people to invest their energy, blood, sweat, and tears.

Hope has a ripple effect we may never fully see. Someone going through a hard time –in your organization or next to you in line at the store—may catch your hope and pass it on.

A leader's visibility gives him or her a multitude of opportunities to motivate people to create a positive, cohesive, healthy, prosperous future. Leaders have more reach, scope, and influence because of the number of people watching, and the world needs more hope-filled leaders.

Hope-filled Future

Historians have defined eras of our past according to the advancements that era developed to improve life. We have the bronze age, the iron age, and the renaissance. More modern eras are known as the industrial age, the machine age, the nuclear age, and the space age. Each time period has offered more and more hope to humanity as we've discovered more efficient methods of working, the value of beauty and art, cures for disease, ease of travel, greater connectedness, and more. I can't possibly finish the list because with each invention and discovery, we unlock the hope for bigger, better, and brighter.

Abundance 360, Singularity University, and other programs have helped me see the extent to which technology has already evolved. However, these types of technology promise to improve exponentially and dramatically impact our way of life. Fifty years ago, only a handful imagined constant connectedness; today, ten-year-olds as well as ninety-year-olds have smartphones. The internet was just emerging when I was a child, today, people discuss the digital landscape on a daily basis. The speed and scope of technology will continue to accelerate, offering the potential to cure every disease or annihilate the earth in two seconds.

These ideas aren't just the realm of science fiction. They could truly come to pass. If we want to live in a future of basic equity, so everyone has food, clean water, and great medical care, we must remain hopefully engaged and inspire others to do the same. Doctors and scientists can do exponentially more than they could ten or twenty years ago. Imagine where we could be in forty years if we develop a hopeful mindset and pass it on to future generations.

We will always need to be smart and analyze risks, but analysis can't override hopeful, inspiring vision that spurs people to action. Hope inspires vision, and vision sees possibilities beyond our wildest imagination.

No one has a crystal ball to know exactly what the future will look like. Thomas Edison hoped we could one day see without a candle. Henry Ford hoped to make travel and distribution easier. Jeff Bezos sends rockets into space, hoping to move damaging industries into space to preserve Earth. Every advancement in history has been born out of hope for a better future.

Hope will allow you to put your brick into the future. Throughout history, France has built many beautiful cathedrals, each one requiring nearly one hundred years to complete. Many who created the designs for these buildings never saw them finished. Three generations of French workers put their bricks into those elaborate structures, believing with all hope that future generations would carry their work to completion. We now have the opportunity to design a future vision or add our brick to the church in the vision another hoped for.

A future of hope won't happen because of a single seminar or speech. That might be where it is born, but hope grows in community where mindsets are changed to appreciate what we have and embrace the potential of what might be.

Hope is born when we learn the first steps in our dance with chaos. Like ballet or line dancing, it's something we practice daily until it becomes a part of our fabric. Just as the motion of our dance builds our body and increases our health, hope gives us energy, strengthens our visionary muscles, and opens a world of possibilities when we engage with it.

Hope does not mean putting on a false smile when the days get dark. It means that even in the darkest times, you have a glimmer inside to encourage you to keep going. When your community sees it's dimming, they bring their light to help you see until you can make it on your own again.

Hope is the foundation of our skill set. We will see it woven into all the others as we move forward. Without hope, it's nearly impossible to face the chaos and dive into the exponential unknown of the future. You'll soon see that hope is one of the building blocks to help us develop courage.

Genie™ Prompts for Hope

Go to www.talk2genie.com and type in one of these conversation starters:

- Let's do a gratitude reflection
- I want to do a future vision exercise
- Help me write positive affirmations
- Let's create goals for a hopeful future
- I want a hope journal

Practical Tips to up your game with HOPE.

Make it real, keep it simple, you're a rock star ☺

These exercises are designed to help you maintain a positive outlook and build resilience in a fast-moving and complex world. Remember that hope is something you can cultivate and strengthen through intentional practice. Developing hope will help you feel rooted and foster optimism in a chaotic world.

Gratitude Dive:
Take a few minutes each day to think about or write down three things you're grateful for. These can be small or big things in your life. Reflect on why you're thankful for them. It's fine to focus on the same things repeatedly or to change them. Whatever you feel grateful for will help shift your focus from what you feel frustrated or worried about to the positive aspects of your life, fostering hope.

Vision Board Dreaming:
Create a vision board or digital collage that represents your aspirations and goals. Dream big. Dream wild. Include images, words, and symbols that inspire hope for your future. Display it where you can see it daily to remind yourself of what you're working towards and the potential for positive change. Take the pressure off by just starting with a few items and then adding to your Vision Board when you feel inspired.

Acts of Kindness:
Engage in random acts of kindness or small acts of generosity regularly. These acts could be as simple as helping a coworker meet a tight deadline, sending a thoughtful message to a friend, or telling a local store worker that you appreciate their helpfulness. Being kind and helpful to others can boost your own sense of hope and well-being. Think of how good it feels to bring a smile to someone else's face, especially when they are not expecting it.

2

Courage

At the height of Nazi Germany, one German-Jewish couple said good-bye to their sixteen-year-old daughter as she boarded a boat to the United States. They were doing what they could to protect her from the horrors of the holocaust. Still, watching their only daughter sail away to an unknown land brought tears and fear. They knew they wouldn't hear from her again until she reached her destination, and even then, communication would be limited, if at all possible. They risked the dangers of sea travel as well as the hardships that faced young ladies traveling alone. Their decision took courage, but they believed their daughter's life depended on it.

I've always admired the bravery of that teen. She left behind everything familiar and accepted a life of uncertainty. Would anyone speak her language when she disembarked?

Would the distant cousins her parents had corresponded with whom she had never met really take care of her? Would this new land look anything like her homeland?

When I took my grandchildren to see the Statue of Liberty, the realization of everything that teen faced hit me hard. You see, that courageous youth was my maternal grandmother. Her boat docked at Ellis Island, so Lady Liberty would have been her first view of this country.

My children and I visited New York in August. To a three- and seven-year-old, the ferry ride was exciting, but I'm not certain they could really comprehend the significance of this New York tourist attraction. As they get older, I'll continue to share the stories of our heritage because I want them to understand the massive and courageous decision their ancestors made to give us the life we have today. They are here because someone had courage to face fear and walk into the unknown.

Courage Births Courage

Some mistake courage for fearlessness. However, fearlessness is foolishness. When we face danger or the unknown, we should have a bit of fear. Fear keeps us vigilant. Courage simply gives us the power to face fear. Merriam-Webster tells us it is the mental or moral strength to venture, persevere, and withstand danger, fear, or difficulty.

The courage of my great-grandparents paved the way for my family, and our bravery opens the door for those who follow us, whether it's family, friends, or your team at work. Courage means making a stand even when it's unpopular. It's having the strength to try with the odds stacked against you. Courageous people face their fears, leave their comfort zone, and take uncomfortable risks.

In business, the one with courage commits to projects they believe in even if there's a chance they might fail. Courage gives you a voice in the times when it would be easier to blend into the background. It takes bravery to explain the benefits of your dream to someone who can't see the exponential picture. Courage asks the hard questions and finds the right person to talk to, even if it means starting at the top.

When we step out of our mold, people will doubt our abilities, and even those who want to support us can sometimes crush our dreams. It takes courage to forge ahead when those we trust can't see our vision. My cousin Lisa recently stepped out courageously to lose eighty pounds in eighteen months. The complete change of lifestyle that kind of commitment takes is a huge step into the unknown. Seeing the doubt in people's eyes when you take on such a big endeavor can be discouraging—a word that literally means to deprive of courage. Lisa's courageous victory now inspires others to venture to that land of greater health and self-confidence.

And that's one of the beautiful things about courage. Courage creates self-confidence. After you conquer that first fear-filled hurdle, you begin to believe you can overcome the next, and with each success, the thing that looked scary, looks smaller and less daunting. In turn, this allows you to face the next trial with a bit more courage than you had the first time. It's not that you don't have fear; rather, you feel as though you have more power to face the fear.

The Consequences of Letting Fear Win

When we start out, the trials can be intimidating. We feel pulled in numerous directions because we haven't yet developed the self-confidence to follow our passion or focus on our own project. It's like a young dancer asked to choreograph her own dance or a musician invited to do a little improv for the first time. Though they know all the moves or notes, they've followed someone else's plan for so long, they can't imagine making the art their own. For each, when the music starts, they'll be tempted to mimic motifs they've danced or played in the past and the more people who watch, the greater the fear of failure. No one likes to appear foolish.

Sadly, some never try. They give up because they fear disappointing the crowd. When I studied theater at Northwestern, I avoided auditioning for some plays because I didn't think I was good enough. I didn't have the courage to go out on that stage and risk looking foolish. Instead, I settled for smaller parts or no part at all.

The same thing happens in business. It's safe to follow someone else's schedule or a program that worked for the last CEO, and for a few, that safe place will bring contentment. However, for the true entrepreneur, lead dancer, and first-chair musician, following someone else's agenda will bring a life of boredom, depression, and lackluster. When we allow intimidation or fear to control our actions, we'll miss the challenge and adventure. It takes courage to live your best life.

The Courageous Write History

Courage is a timeless theme. In fact, history books are filled with accounts of bravery and the willingness to go against the grain to make a difference. Socrates refused to abandon the philosophical ideas that shaped the way we think and process knowledge today. Even after being arrested and threatened with death, he courageously held to his convictions.

Many know about Paul Revere, but few know of sixteen-year-old Sybil Ludington, who risked her life to ride forty miles in the middle of the night to warn revolutionary

Americans that the British were coming. And Casper ten Boom and his family hid countless Jews and aided in their escape during the holocaust. His daughter, Corrie, rose to fame after sharing her story about becoming her family's lone survivor following their arrest and imprisonment in a concentration camp.

I can't begin to list all the men and women who risked everything to bring freedom, adventure, and our comfortable way of life. Even today, every major improvement or discovery comes because someone dares to step outside of conventional thinking, walk in places uncomfortable or unfamiliar, or face the unknown.

Building Muscles of Courage

I've had to be courageous on more than one occasion to get where I am today. After finishing high school, I courageously pursued a career field that few break into. I went into acting with no back up plan, and even though I didn't stay in that field for long, I learned I could fall short of my goals and still be a success. Trying is a success all its own. Courage is a tremendous teacher even when we don't complete the original plan.

More than twenty years ago, after graduating from college, I moved from the familiarity of the United States to Europe. Those first years in France were an intense mix of wonder and discovery coupled with profound doubt. I didn't know anyone. I faced intense family pressure to come home. I was trying to break into French acting and theater with a noticeable American accent, thus limiting roles for which I could audition. I had limited financial resources from my day job teaching English to business executives. The list goes on and on. It took courage to follow my heart, stick it out, and find a way forward.

Courage also helped me start my business and overcome the operational challenges every entrepreneur faces. It has pushed me to keep going even when things looked bleak with the exponential growth of technology and the ever-changing systems of business. The courage I built during those adventures saw me through as I rallied through the COVID epidemic and reinvented my business while raising two young children.

The stories of building courage are endless. Helen Keller faced the fear of a dark and silent world. I can't imagine how she felt when Anne Sullivan, a total stranger, forced her into the world of signing letters. The more the young girl accomplished, the stronger her courage grew, until she became a prominent advocate for the hearing and seeing impaired communities. Though she couldn't see or hear her audience, she bravely communicated to thousands her message of hope and courage and changed the world's perception of disabilities.

Each time I've had to exercise courage to complete a task, it strengthened that muscle. The more I complete, the more I believe I can complete the next task. Even failure bolsters courage because it teaches us that looking foolish isn't as deadly as we think. It's like a ballerina learning pointe. The first time she raises to her toes, it's painful, but the more she does it, the stronger her legs become until finally her pirouettes and leaps look effortless.

Dancing With Chaos Takes Courage

Dancing with the chaos of today's exponential changes requires courage. One hundred years ago, people spent their entire life building their knowledge. Most stayed in the same career field for sixty years, and the lessons of their youth provided a great foundation for what came later. Each year added more bricks to their building.

The fast-paced changes of the twenty-first century mean starting from scratch again and again. Today, people change jobs an average of twelve times during their working years, and 52% of the working population consider a complete career change on any given day. And given the fact that 9% of the population has a downright phobia of change. [9] [10] and 71% say they fear it, facing the shifting culture of the exponential curve will require extra bravery. In one poll, eight out of ten people admitted they'd "missed out on golden opportunities" because the fear of the unknown held them back. [11]

When we understand we're not alone in our fear, it can help push us out of our comfort zone. In fact, if we step out in courage, we'll find that many of the people who intimidate us because they seem to be tremendously successful actually admire us. They, too, have faced the scary prospect of starting over. They know what it's like to get back up after failure. So, when they watch you forge into the unknown or the uncomfortable, they're cheering you on. And honestly, if they aren't, you probably don't want to work with or try to impress them anyway.

One of the best things about building your muscle of courage and acting bravely is the hope that it brings to others. Yes, these basic principles of dancing with chaos are intrinsically linked. Hope builds courage, and courage builds hope. And not just for you. Others watching you demonstrate courage even when you fail will also have hope. And as you gain courage and instill hope, you'll also see the beauty of your increased focus.

Genie™ Prompts for Courage

Go to www.talk2genie.com and type in one of these conversation starters:

- Let's do a courage reflection
- Help me write courage affirmations
- Suggest some small acts of courage
- Build a fear confrontation plan
- I want to visualize overcoming a fear
- Help me make a courageous decision

Practical Tips to up your game with COURAGE.

Make it real, keep it simple, you're a rock star ☺

These exercises combine mindfulness, gradual exposure, and self-reflection to help you develop courage and a sense of rootedness in an intensely accelerating and unpredictable world. By facing your fears, practicing courage, and using affirmations, you can increase your resilience and confidence in uncertain situations.

Step Out of Your Comfort Zone:
Regularly challenge yourself to step out of your comfort zone in small ways. This could be speaking up in a meeting, taking on a new responsibility at work, or initiating a difficult conversation. Every uncomfortable act builds courage and confidence to tackle larger challenges. Each time you step out of your comfort zone, take a moment to congratulate yourself for doing so. It is important to recognize your courage regardless of the specific outcome from your new move.

Take a moment now to think about an upcoming situation where you can step out of your comfort zone. Once you have identified the situation, put it in your calendar so you can commit to doing it.

Confront Your Fears:
Identify one fear or anxiety that's been holding you back from reaching a goal you really care about. Commit to facing it gradually. Start with small steps to confront this fear, and gradually increase the challenge as you become more comfortable. This practice desensitizes you to the fear and helps you develop the courage to handle it effectively. It will make you feel more rooted and capable of handling the challenges and doubts you face.

Daily Affirmations:
Create a list of daily affirmations focused on courage and resilience. Repeat these affirmations to yourself each morning or whenever you need a boost of confidence. Examples include "I am brave and capable," "I embrace challenges with courage," and "I am resilient in the face of adversity." If you want even stronger results with this exercise, look in the mirror and say it out loud to yourself. You might feel a little funny with this one at the beginning, but it works wonders! In addition to developing your courage, this practice also helps you build a closer relationship with yourself.

3

Focus

Focus involves directing attention to a specific activity, person, or event. It's one of the basic rooting principles because focus is driven by purpose. And as we mentioned before, defining our purpose is essential.

The concept of focus used to escape me. Don't get me wrong, I had no problem with concentration. I could concentrate anywhere, at any time, for long periods of time with no problem. But concentration and focus aren't necessarily the same thing.

Until I joined Strategic Coach in 2021, I spent fifteen-and-a-half years following the fire in my belly. Whatever idea struck me, I followed it. Without a defined purpose, I didn't know what to focus my concentration on, and I had no goal to filter my to-do list through. Like many entrepreneurs, I lacked an efficient and effective way to focus. I often took on too much. I knew that concentrating on fewer projects allowed me to complete things with better results. However, I got frustrated when I realized I missed so many other cool things. I wanted to do everything!

Studying with Strategic Coach(R) taught me the difference between focus and concentration. True focus fixates on the right things—the things that serve your larger vision and purpose. Though the concept seems logical and not hard to comprehend, it can be much more difficult to systematize and put into practice. Strategic Coach brings together groups of driven and successful entrepreneurs, so there's a wealth of experience, spirit, and wisdom. Listening to others' successes and struggles has given me a valuable mirror to help me understand my business, my team members, my clients, myself, and our results on a much deeper level.

Begin at the End

We can't truly focus until we know what we are passionate about. Defining our purpose and asking what we want the end-result to look like is imperative. Then we can begin to narrow down the things we're willing to do to reach our destination.

After we've determined what the end will look like, we have two options. Will we do the work ourselves or delegate?

If we decide to be hands-on, we have to figure out some way to avoid being nearsighted. We can get so hung up on small details, we miss the big picture and miss serving our best, largest possible vision. That's why focus is important, it tells us where to put our concentration.

If, instead, we opt to delegate, we start by making sure the person who will handle the project has the method we expect them to use, if any. And we'll need a plan that we can use to initiate our representative.

As we plan the end, we have to determine the long-, medium-, short-, and immediate-term goals, and we have to know how to toggle between them. Unfortunately, the complexity and speed of the current world can get us off track if we become nearsighted regarding the immediate- or short-term goals without keeping the end in focus. Without that end-goal constantly in our sights, we find ourselves concentrating on something smaller than our potential.

Many of us don't push ourselves beyond what we can easily see because it's a difficult exercise. Understanding the steps is deceivingly simple. We begin by creating a big, vivid picture of our long-term results. Then, we break the plan into short-term action-based goals. Each of these small goals are merely stepping stones that take us to our main purpose.

Even though the process is that simple, embracing that thought-space and executing such an uncomplicated plan isn't easy. Most of us have been putting fires out for so long, it's difficult to break the habit. We could make significant progress if we consistently carved out two hours every week for vision planning, but these two hours feel expendable when the fires break out.

Developing focus gives you permission to say no. You might find a way to fix a problem, but when you compare it to the plan of the larger vision, it doesn't fit. Jumping into action can be tempting, but cultivating a new thought process that allows us to begin with the phrase, "No, wait," frees us to reach our goals and live our purpose.

Each time we're tempted to act in haste, we need to ask, "Will this decision serve me years down the road, or will I get knocked off course in the heat of the moment?"

Sharing Your Focus

It's rare for individuals and organizations to approach vision setting in sufficient detail to achieve true focus. While some of the top management among my clients have an extremely clear vision that reveals itself in the company culture, it's more common for leaders to have admirable methods that don't trickle down. Clarity at the top level that doesn't reach every area of the organization lowers the chance of reaching goals. Success requires focus and clear-cut understanding across the board. In the absence of focus and purpose, you're likely to miss the mark, only partially meet your goal, or expend unnecessary energy.

Before I defined my focus, I generally just took the most logical fork in the road. In hindsight, I realized I would have been better off adapting to fit a bigger vision. I had concentration and adaptability without the benefit of peak focus. The company worked and grew, but we could have even better. Focus and clarity drive the choices at those inflection points to ensure your overall arc continues in the right direction.

In most entrepreneurships today, everyone manages or participates in a variety of different projects. Without clarity on the key projects and a definition of the key result, we'll waste and misdirect our energy. No one can focus two hundred percent on every project, so we need to narrow our focus and prioritize our list. Creating a vision and setting a focal point helps us avoid getting swept away.

Focus Creates a Need for Adjustments

My business is constantly adapting and reinventing. If we didn't have clarity and focus, those adaptations could cause distractions and keep us from reaching our true purpose. By defining the things that are most important, we know what to concentrate on in the midst of these transformations and distractions.

Just like turning the ring around the lens of a camera sharpens the image, as we develop focus, our purpose will become more and more clear. And when we apply the same principles of discovering purpose and focus to other areas of life, we can see success there, too.

My children top my list of focus, followed by running my business. I give energy and care to other aspects of my life as well, but defining those two points as my primary passions makes it easy for me to filter out the things that won't enhance my life vision.

The focus I give my children feels very different from my business focus, but the underlying skill is the same. Focusing on my family means spending time with my kids, instilling important values in them, and ensuring they are happy, healthy, and learning in their environment. I have long-term goals related to their education and helping them find their own purpose and vision.

Having two major focus points means my time gets split between my family and my business, but the time isn't always evenly divided. For instance, when my children were born, my focus shifted to giving birth and caring for a newborn.

Prior to having children, I spent more time with my friends. I still love them, but being a mother meant reducing my socializing. Making those adjustments and balancing my family and my business is a dance of its own. Sometimes the children lead, and other times it's the business. And when the song breaks, I can spend a minute with my friends.

By defining a purpose in your business as well as other important areas in your life, you will better be able to discern how to focus as well as allocate your time and energy accordingly.

You might have one, two, or more areas of focus. I have a brilliant, talented coach on my team who I've worked with for fifteen years. One of her primary focuses is not being overextended or rushed. I've witnessed her skillfully shift and adapt her focus many times. She does it by clearly communicating her vision, her priorities, and her limits and by respecting herself enough to let her actions reflect that. She admires my professional accomplishments but parcels her focus in a different way. This coach has chosen three or four focus areas, and she adjusts as necessary.

The number of your primary foci isn't important, but it is vital that you identify them, so you know how to proceed. The dance becomes tiring and confusing when we spread ourselves thin, trying to devote time to every possible pursuit. A large, clear vision will narrow our focus and help us set limits so we can be our best selves in each area that we've defined as a priority.

Creating this lifestyle of focus will attract people with similar qualities. The dynamic becomes a virtuous circle as you feed off each other's energy and build on each other's skills. By the same token, if you don't cultivate focus, you may push away the people you actually want to attract, whether personally or professionally.

Defining your focus, clarity, and purposeful values may make you realize your child's school doesn't align with those values. You then make decisions based on this new perspective.

I shared my own story of deepening my understanding of focus through Strategic Coach because I encourage everyone to reassess the way they understand fulfilling their vision. So many of us know how to concentrate or have a modicum of focus, but we could go much deeper.

Regardless of your current level of focus, you can continue to refine it. Taking the time to define your purpose and revisiting it on regular intervals will help you hone the skill set.

Focused Leadership

In a team setting, clarifying the long-term vision and creating operational steps ensures everyone moves in the same direction. When leaders communicate the process to the team and then demonstrate focus by not allowing the conversation to get pulled off track, we create a space that fosters collaboration, and we enable team members to step into greater leadership roles.

This strategy allows our company to raise leaders who share our vision. By providing clarity for each project, our leaders can move projects forward with more efficiency. Each leader is like the captain of a dance troupe or the lead of a waltz couple. Their every move tells the rest of the team which direction to take. Providing clear cues in business is every bit as vital as the cues a waltz partner provides. And being the one who follows and reads those cues accurately is no less valuable. When the purpose is clearly communicated, and the leader demonstrates focus that can be easily followed, a project can be completed with the beauty of a synchronized ballet.

In his book Traction, Gino Wickman likens a business team to a row team. It's imperative that all rowers keep their oars moving similarly, focused on the same destination. With each contemporaneous stroke, the boat glides through the water faster and faster. Their synchrony creates efficiency. Similar alignments create an amazing capacity to get things done.

Many think that taking time to clarify their vision and the steps to achieve their purpose will slow them down, but these simple actions actually turbocharge your ability to achieve. It's easy for individuals and organizations to get sidetracked in the craziness. But focusing on the dance, the leader, and the beauty of the moment can propel us to achieve our greater purpose.

Apply Focus to Keep from Spinning Out of Control

When a prima ballerina performs the perfect pirouette, she focuses on one point as she turns, with every spin, her head twists as needed to keep her eyes on that focal point. If her eyes followed her body, she would get dizzy and fall over, but with a definitive focus she can stay balanced on one toe and keep the spin going for as long as the music dictates, a feat that causes awe to fall over the audience.

Concentration has always been a part of my life. My dad once watched me as I wrote. He commented that it seemed like I just flipped a switch and my concentration turned on. Whether I'm acting, writing, or preparing a keynote speech, I'm driven, and that drive keeps me in the moment. I refined my company's marketing with my highly driven concentration. But focusing on the current task didn't protect me from the dizziness of flitting from project to project.

The game changed when Strategic Coach challenged my understanding of focus. I learned that my semi-specific purpose and ability to concentrate weren't sufficient to take me where I wanted to go. Thanks to my new understanding, I've learned to marshal my inner strength to craft a clearer vision and articulate it to my team. When everyone understands our values and what we're doing within those values we can increase morale. And when the entire team begins to see where we want to be next year and how that will propel us to our goal in ten years, everyone gets on board with the vision.

We cannot control the instability of the world. But we can control our portion of the dance. Focus, along with a clear purpose, allows us to connect to what we see as most important. It allows us to communicate why it's important and helps us allocate each team member's energy to maximize our efforts and reach our goals. Focus roots us and feeds our inner peace and sense of stability. As the world twirls at an ever-increasing rate, our focal point will keep us balanced, and while the rest of the planet feels like everything is spinning out of control, our pirouette will be beautiful, timed perfectly, and full of focus.

Genie™ Prompts for Focus

Go to www.talk2genie.com and type in one of these conversation starters:

- Help me with improving my daily focus
- Let's create a focus plan
- I want to eliminate distractions
- Build a morning focus ritual
- Help me with maintain focus during tasks
- Let's create a focus-friendly environment

Practical Tips to up your game with FOCUS.

Make it real, keep it simple, you're a rock star ☺

These exercises can significantly improve your ability to maintain focus in a world filled with distractions and uncertainty. Regular practice will help you stay on track and achieve your goals more effectively.

Pomodoro Technique:
Use the Pomodoro Technique to enhance your focus and productivity. Set a timer for 25 minutes (a "Pomodoro"), during which you work on a specific task with full concentration. After the Pomodoro, take a 5-minute break. Repeat this cycle, and after completing four Pomodoros, take a longer break of

15-30 minutes. This method helps you maintain focus. The fact that it is timed and that you know you will get a break can also help to motivate you when you are procrastinating. It can dedramatize something that you are feeling intimidated about doing. In short, this practice is great to get you focused and moving forward.

Goal Visualization:
Spend time each day visualizing your long-term goals and the life you aspire to have. Create a mental picture of your objectives, imagining the details and emotions associated with achieving them. This exercise helps reinforce your commitment to your vision and motivates you to take focused actions to bring it to reality.

Regular Progress Review:
Set aside a specific time each week or month or quarter to review your progress toward your life vision and key objectives. Reflect on what you've accomplished, what needs adjustment, and any challenges you've encountered. This exercise helps you remain aligned with your goals and make necessary course corrections. Find the frequency that works the best for you! Even reviewing your goals and life vision once a year will be significantly more impactful than not at all!

4

Strong Relationships

We live in an era that allows for more personal connections than ever before. When my grandmother left
Germany, she lost contact with her family for a long
time. Between the distance, the speed with which letters
could travel, and limitations put in place by the Nazi regime,
communication was difficult.

Today, our friends go on vacation across an ocean, and
we follow their every move, either literally—if they have a
GPS tracker enabled—or through social media posts. Still,
it doesn't take a research team to convince us we're the most
disconnected generation of all time. Between remote work,
cyber-bullying, and the trend to look down at our phones,
more people feel isolated and alone than ever before.

We face information overload, bombarded with 100,500
words and twelve hours of information and media every day.

[12]But filling up on all that information still leaves us empty. Despite all the advancements, information, and exponential growth at our fingertips, the truth is humans need other humans. Strong relationships steady and root us. We move forward best when we surround ourselves with people who support and care about us.

Building a Tribe

The term tribe has become very trendy, but we've really come full circle. The earliest civilizations record social groups that formed for support, protection, and to avoid loneliness. The Scots and Irish called them clans, in Africa and the Americas they're referred to as tribes, and Eastern United States, hill people referred to their close-knit group as kinfolk. Though we've moved away from the front porch mentality of the early 1900s, humanity has begun to recognize the importance of having a group of caring souls to lean on.

Strong relationships create community and expand our potential. In the Amish communities of Ohio and Pennsylvania, huge barns are built in a day without power tools because the entire community comes together to support one family. And in the business world, offices that provide a community environment and encourage collaboration rather than competition see a fifty percent increase in productivity.

[13]I've benefited from belonging to a tribe in every stage of my life. From my summer camp experience as a child to my theater troupes in college and, more recently, Abundance360 and Strategic Coach, I've developed connections that have carried me to places I may have never gone on my own.

In addition to the support that a community can bring, it also offers extreme mental and physical health benefits.

Studies reveal isolation provides a higher risk of heart disease and stroke as well as a forty percent increase in the risk of dementia. One study showed that being alone can heighten health risks to the same levels as smoking fifteen cigarettes a day or having an alcohol use disorder. Plus, it's twice as deadly as obesity.[14] Humans need to feel connected.

We all get to the place where we feel like throwing in the towel. But when those feelings persist, it's often from a lack of community. I can point to times when I didn't have proper support systems in place. My tribes have given me perseverance.

Strong Relationships

Tribal community is more than two people in the same room together. And the strength and depth of the relationship will depend on its nature. A boss/employee relationship will look vastly different than two team members who share responsibility for a project. However, any relationship can provide connectedness when each person feels as though the other cares about his or her well-being.

Relationships that offer mutual trust and caring and replenish your energy make for strong connections. The most important aspect is the give and take in the pairing. Much like a couple dancing, the two have to move together, back and forth. If one person constantly pulls the other or becomes dependent on his or her partner to carry the weight, the performance becomes stiff, and both people grow weary.

Some tremendously strong relationships are built between clients and providers. Though my client relationships are different from my friendships outside of work, I feel close to many I serve. The nuances of those business relationships mirror the relationships I have with friends even though we don't socialize outside of work. We set healthy boundaries and respectful communication. We genuinely care about each other, and our sense of dedication and commitment grows. Our bond goes beyond caring for a project or a service.

Business relationships differ because we also have a contract to respect. In some ways this strengthens the relationship because with a good contract in place, we know what to expect from one another. A business that creates that community with clients is called client-centric; however, like any strong relationship, when the attitude of community is authentic, the business benefits as much from the connection as the client. It's no wonder this kind of organization is becoming so successful. The trust these relationships build is the most effective way to distinguish yourself in this overstimulated fast-moving world.

Evaluating Relationships

In today's business landscape, it's important to remember there are others who can provide high quality service to your clients. What they can't provide is your personality and your connection. When problems arise—and they will—connected clients are more willing to express dissatisfaction and work with us to create a solution. Without the relationship, it's easier for them to go find another provider.

Likewise, not every client is for you. Constant conflict is draining, and some clients don't want to build those strong relationships that help us weather the storms. Those kinds of people deplete our focus, energy, creativity, and capacity to collaborate. It's a cost we can't afford in this world of exponential change.

When evaluating relationships, it's good to step back and ask yourself whether that connection energizes you or drains you. Do you feel lifted, or are you always the one doing the lifting? Does that group or individual help you dance through the chaos or bring more confusion?

On the other hand, we don't want to mistake constructive criticism for conflict. When someone you trust brings a problem to your attention, it might sting, but ultimately, they are offering you an opportunity to grow. Brutal honesty can be hurtful in the moment; however, when we realize it's couched in genuine concern for our best interest, we need to embrace that relationship. Those are the kinds of people who will help you find the best you. They'll keep you on track toward your vision.

Weathering Turmoil

Nearly any relationship can weather turmoil with a clear, compelling, shared commitment. Strong relationships can withstand challenges. Personal and professional relationships have different characteristics, but loyalty and perseverance are essential to both. I think about all the difficult situations my clients have faced through the years—budget cuts, layoffs, and so on. A good part of the strength in these relationships stems from my genuine desire to have their backs and empathize with their hardship. Sticking around when the road gets rough has a lasting impact on a relationship.

We've all experienced difficult stretches and felt the surprise when a close friend or family member didn't support us. Those missteps hurt deeply and are hard to move past. If the connection doesn't have a grounding in conflict resolution, acknowledgment, taking ownership, and making amends, it's hard for a relationship to stay intact. But if you value a relationship, you'll be there when your friend is going through difficult times.

Our company often talks about sweating with our clients. If something unexpected happens or goes wrong, we sweat it out with them. We work together on the solution. That mutual effort and investment builds a deep connection and fosters loyalty. When you walk with someone through the valley, they're more likely to stay with you.

The Personal Connection

I'm sure you've worked with someone you felt you couldn't depend on. Learning how to interact with a mass diversity of personalities can be an adventure. We end up picking up the slack or worrying that their portion of the project won't get done. Often, you'll find yourself anxious as the project grows to a close, fearful someone dropped the ball, and the whole juggling act will come crashing down.

If you have a perfectionist personality, you might have to make sure your expectations are realistic; however, if you're the kind that works best under pressure, perhaps it's time to step up your game to keep others from feeling the stress of last stretch finishes. Great relationships look for the other person's point of view and attempt to work within the scope of both personalities. When this happens in a give and take scenario, relationships deepen, and everyone feels more confident.

Communication is key in these more stressful connections. We can't expect people to know what we're thinking. As hard as they try to see things through our lens, it can't be done, so it's vital we give them our perspective.

It's equally important to listen to theirs. True listening may be the most valuable of communication skills. It means paying attention to body language, tone, and demeanor, as well as using our own physical cues to let them know they're heard. Listening entails genuine interest in what the other person is saying, showing them how much you value their contribution.

Relationships deepen when we are present in the moment. One of the most tempting parts of conversation is focusing on your next remark while the other person is talking. Everyone does it, and it's addressed in all sorts of communication exercises, but at the risk of repeating something you've already heard, I'll say it. It's critical to remove yourself from the next statement and remain in the present.

Communication also includes honesty, and sometimes that means constructive observations. We have to learn how to receive those as well as give them. When others discover you always give an honest, fair, and respectful opinion even when it's unpopular and can also handle having your opinion dismissed, they will respect everything you say. Your words will carry more weight than those who sugar coat or always agree. Clients, in particular, will want to work with you because they'll know you're always giving them your best advice, not the most digestible.

Finally, personal connection means you take an interest in the details of someone else's life. You pay attention to dates on the calendar and ask about their vacation. If they've been off for two days because of a sick child, you ask how they're doing before you dive into the business. Paying attention when they talk about their spouse or children and remembering those names will make people understand that you care.

Franklin D. Roosevelt amazed his staff because he remembered the names of nearly everyone he met. [15] Can you imagine the impact that would make on the individual he spoke to for only a few minutes? People appreciate being seen as a whole person rather than a project or a speck in time.

Choose Relationships Carefully

Carefully choosing the people with whom I have a close relationship may be the number one key to my strong community. Some qualities I look for are positive energy, forward-moving, kind, non-manipulative, and sharing my vibration. I want to be around people who fill me up rather than drag me down. The world has enough complaining. So, while everyone needs to vent from time to time, we don't want negativity to become the focus of our input or output.

My capacity for relationships is finite. While I'd love to connect with everyone, there just isn't room, so I want to be certain the people I develop a close bond with enrich my life and help me grow. I also want to be able to provide this for others. You don't have to look for people who are more intelligent, more accomplished, or have more money than you—if they have a proactive stance toward the world, you can enrich each other by going deep and sharing trust.

British anthropologist Robin Dunbar and his associates conducted a number of studies on our capability to maintain relationships. "Dunbar's number," as his scale has become known, estimates that each person can successfully maintain approximately one hundred fifty meaningful contacts, fifteen close friends, and five intimate friends. [16] His work in this field demonstrates our need to be a bit choosy about who we bring into our inner circle.

Though I want a diverse community, I find great value in connections with people who understand what I'm going through and share my values. Strategic Coach has been instrumental in strengthening my relational foundation by surrounding me with inspiring, positive-minded entrepreneurs at various points in their business journeys.

Feeling understood made an enormous difference in my growth as a leader. Brain surgeons need at least a few close relationships with people who have a hands-on understanding of the intense responsibility of that job. The same goes for entrepreneurs or any other profession. Even being a mother can benefit from strong relationships with others who have a passion to help their children reach their full potential.

Strong Relationships Root You

One strong relationship undergirded me when I started my company. My father can be a tough customer. He's not an easygoing person, nor is he generous with compliments. He was hard on me at times during my childhood, and he still calls a spade a spade.

Even so, I can count on him to acknowledge my accomplishments. On those days when I feel like I should have done twenty times more, my dad points out how much I've accomplished by taking care of my family, cooking dinner, and writing a proposal. He praises me for juggling the kids and my business and for raising two children on my own without full-time help. He notices that I never complain. His recognition and support mean the world to me.

In our mutually beneficial, give and take relationship, his praise and support also makes him feel good because my success reflects on him since he raised me. That's how strong relationships work. It's never just one person winning while the other loses.

Strong relationships naturally find balance with everyone working toward a common goal. It's like a dance company moving together to make certain everyone shines. Each relationship we cultivate has the potential to enrich us, and nothing can replace the support and encouragement we feel when we connect with people who understand what we're going through without much explanation. People who have developed strong connections have more hope and courage. Being part of communities that offer hope as part of their DNA has paid off in more ways than I can count. Today, people see me as a high-energy, optimistic, hope-filled person, and I appreciate each person in my family, my team, and my tribe who have helped me along the journey.

Genie™ Prompts for Strong Relationships

Go to www.talk2genie.com and type in one of these conversation starters:

- Help me with improve my communication skills
- Let's create a plan to strengthen my relationships
- I want to build trust with my colleagues
- Create a strategy to resolve conflicts effectively
- I want to build a network of supportive relationships
- Practice and enhance my empathy skills
- I want to improve my relationship with my partner

Practical Tips to up your game with STRONG RELATIONSHIPS.

Make it real, keep it simple, you're a rock star ☺

These exercises help nurture and strengthen your relationships, providing a source of support and stability in the face of the challenges presented in a fast-changing and complex world. They promote open communication, quality time, and emotional connection, all of which are essential for thriving relationships in uncertain times.

Digital Detox Time:
Dedicate specific days or just periods of time (like meals for example) for digital detox, where you disconnect from screens and devices. Use this time to focus on spending quality, uninterrupted time with your loved ones. Engage in face-to-face conversations, outdoor activities, or simply enjoy a meal together. Digital detox can help you deepen your connections in a world filled with digital distractions.

Empathy Mode vs. Challenging Mode:
In a strong relationship, Empathy Mode and Challenging Mode serve distinct and valuable roles. Knowing when to favor one mode over the other can really help you develop your relationships and tune in to others' needs and growth.

Empathy involves actively listening and understanding the person's emotions and experiences, providing comfort and support. It's essential during times of vulnerability when validation and compassion are needed.

On the other hand, Challenging Mode involves respectfully questioning or discussing differing viewpoints, behaviors, reactions, decisions, interpretations. It's appropriate when growth, problem-solving, or promoting healthy change is the goal.

Striking the right balance between Empathy and Challenging mode depends on the situation, as both approaches contribute to the depth and resilience of the relationship.

3 Points of View:
Conflicts are inevitable in any relationship, especially in a chaotic and shifting world. The Point of View (POV) conflict resolution technique can be easily applied.

Start by examining a conflict from three distinct perspectives: your own viewpoint, the other person's perspective, and that of an objective observer. By projecting into and empathizing with each viewpoint, you gain a deeper understanding of the conflict's dynamics.

POV Conflict Resolution will help facilitate more effective communication and resolution. This technique encourages empathy, open-mindedness, and the potential for finding common ground in challenging situations. It can help take away the anger or rage you may be feeling since you will also identify with other perspectives.

5

Creativity

A rcheology has uncovered countless cave drawings, hiero-glyphics, and beautifully crafted characters that formed early means of communication and art. The creative nature of our ancestors allows these scientists to date each layer in their digs. They decorated pottery and formed it in such unique ways, archeologists can identify the dates and cultures who lived in those areas. Creativity rooted these ancient civilizations, and it is no less important today.

Creativity and the Exponential Curve

Creativity and the exponential curve relate to each other much like the chicken and the egg. Does the exponential curve drive creativity, or does creativity drive the exponential curve? Throughout history, creativity has driven cultural advancements which have inspired more creativity.

I work in the area of dialectic methods. The ancient Greeks codified the process during an intense period of their history two thousand years ago. Social and political norms, as well as the face of democracy, were rapidly changing. The transforming culture created an arena for creative, diverse debate to minimize conflict and expedite the exchange of ideas and discovery of the best solutions.

Like dialectic methods, navigating this exponentially changing culture means understanding that competing opinions can lead to creative solutions. When we use dialectic methods, we explore ideas, investigate truths, ask questions, and build on the original ideas to creatively find a unified answer.

Cultivating creativity will help you navigate the complexities of today's world. As a manager, you might be facing a major deadline while simultaneously forced to replace a majority of the project team. On top of that, the ever-changing culture could make your product irrelevant before you have a chance to launch. Challenges and changes in parameters arise all the time. Success requires being able to creatively adapt.

Creativity and Diversity

Diversity also breeds creativity, and creativity feeds diversity. As we invite unfamiliar cultures and thinking into our world, we'll also welcome competing and confrontational ideas. History gives us countless examples of how to successfully or unsuccessfully navigate this introduction of diversity. Though much of the world didn't appreciate Rome invading their nations, the culture, roadways, and architecture that stemmed from the merging of cultures lives on today.

As we add diversity to our communities, we'll have to adapt to cultural and language differences. Plus, adding diversity to our tribe challenges us to learn new things and grow.

While most reserve the word creative to describe artists, musicians, dancers, crafters, and thespians, learning and adapting is a form of creativity as well. Learning and adapting force us to think outside the box. Changing yourself is just as creative as performing improv.

The concept of diversity is so much bigger than culture and ethnicity. People whose main goal is to climb a corporate ladder are threatened by those with diverse ideas, innovations, and inventions. Will their imagination offer a bigger or better solution to the company problem? And these innovators could build on our idea until it becomes something we don't even recognize.

Without grounding, this dance between diversity and creativity turns into chaos. People feel defensive, apprehensive, and confrontational, causing creativity to shut down for fear of making waves or getting fired. Because the creatives feel as though they are wasting their time and talents, they'll eventually move on, and without creativity, the tribe will crumble from within.

In contrast, those who root themselves in creativity relish in the expansion of their ideas. They realize they can become a part of amazing breakthroughs that benefit the entire organization. The old adage says, "Necessity is the mother of invention." However, that's only a partial truth. Creativity is the mother of invention; necessity provides the inspiration. Since the beginning of time, creatives have been finding solutions to problems before much of the population knew a problem existed.

When Edison perfected the ideas of the many who'd gone before him, some didn't understand the need. They hadn't seen the problem because candles and oil lamps were taking care of the problem fine as far as they were concerned. If not for a diverse group of these creative minds, we might still be sitting around fires.

Many don't realize the depth of diversity's roots within our civilization. My company's multicultural seminars are amongst the most profound programs we run. This rooting in creativity coupled with diversity creates changed mindsets that frees people to enjoy the dance. By grounding ourselves in the need for diversity in creativity, we can move confidently in the chaos of this changing world.

Foster Creativity

In addition to promoting diversity, my company also runs programs to foster creativity or inclusivity. People leave with a strong sense of belonging within a company accompanied by solid product-development strategies and client-relationship practices. But bigger than these organizational skills, I find our participants experience the most powerful change at a deeper and more personal level. They shift their mindset, and the perspective of their surroundings changes.

A palpable energy and joy fill the room at these gatherings. The bath of creativity, with ideas bouncing off the walls, creates genuinely happy faces. They look like they just got engaged, promoted, or closed a big deal. We can see the energetic power of deep connection to the creativity that roots them in our environment and universe.

We use the famous dot exercise as a visual to help participants see how simple creativity can make a difference. The goal is to connect nine dots laid out in a square using only four lines and without lifting the pen or retracing their route.

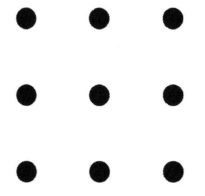

Instructions:
Get a pen and paper and copy the nine dots arranged in a square below.
To solve the puzzle, you need to join all nine dots by drawing no more than four straight lines.
The straight lines must be continuous – meaning you must not lift your pen from the paper once you start drawing.
You will find the answer to the puzzle at the end of the book.

Even with one hundred people in the room, only a few will be able to complete the task, because the only way to succeed is to break out of the square. Though frameless, most assume an imaginary boundary, and they trap themselves inside.

The analogy is powerful. How often do we limit our creativity because we put constraints upon ourselves—constraints built in our mind. The key to creativity is recognizing there is no box. There never was a box. By removing the boxes in our minds, we cultivate creativity and allow for a diversity of perspectives and solutions.

When we get stuck or feel like our creativity is stifled, we need to ask two questions:

1. Can I go outside the box?

2. Is there even a box?

We do another exercise with clients in high-level sales. We invite them to respond to the most difficult client objections that arise in complex negotiations, which may or may not be in good faith. For example, objections may be an excuse to get rid of the service provider.

Most sales teams don't know how to respond when a client says, "You talk a great deal about innovation. I don't see anything innovative in your offer." Or, "Why would we have a different experience with you this time, when five years ago, the project was late and not finished correctly?" Even experienced, high-performing salespeople tend to freeze in such situations.

We help participants learn how to manage the tribal mentality of self-preservation. If we can avoid the "us vs. them" mentality when someone attacks in the middle of a meeting, the outcome can be drastically different. Putting the conversation in a framework that is to their advantage before they respond helps promote their message and allows them to move forward. Clients figure out, creatively, which framework would be advantageous for both them and their clients.

If you're in the right mindset, there are a plethora of ways to move forward while preserving what's most important to your plan. You'll naturally find a framework that fits. When you practice generating multiple creative, positive possibilities, you develop the confidence to think on your feet, even in tough negotiations, and the fear starts to fall away.

In creativity workshops, people often have the fear of saying something stupid or coming up with a "bad" idea. We emphasize that getting stuck in the good-bad binary forces them to look for the one "right" answer and kills creativity. To stoke creativity, we dig until we get all the ideas out. The goal is to become highly comfortable and confident in the ability to find multiple possibilities. We only probe for possibilities for about twenty minutes, allowing the team to build the necessary element of speed. Quick, flexible creativity serves complex client situations.

In keeping up with the pace of our world, it's important to remember there are always multiple ways out. Objections are opportunities, and those challenging moments with a client can become inspirational, creative moments. Your ability to respond creatively may be precisely what makes them buy your service, renew the contract, or stay loyal to you.

Finally, we help teams learn to excel in creative thinking and collective intelligence. Brainstorming, for example, is the most basic form of a lateral creativity method. Vertical or restrictive creativity methods involve setting constraints which can generate a higher quality of ideas; however, it poses challenges and typically makes it more difficult to work through as an exercise. Vertical thinking often includes repetitive sequences with a timed framework. This generates revision after revision at a very fast pace.

A lateral exercise will invite you to take five minutes to list all the ways in which you can improve your client's experience during the project, while a vertical exercise will give you a change in parameters. For instance, your project that was supposed to be accomplished in three months with a team of twenty will now be due in three weeks with a team of five. How can you fit the project into the new box and still meet the expectations of the client?

While lateral methods get your brain thinking in an open and creative way, the tougher scenario of the vertical method will drive innovation.

Our Leader Lab teaches a variety of collaborative and creative problem solving methods, based on a principle known as co-development, which allows groups of people to work on real ideas in different roles and scenarios. We use various forms of creativity, including the techniques of Edward de Bono, the originator of lateral thinking. We built this structured group creativity method primarily for senior management. It helps the leaders quickly and collaboratively find responses to various problems, questions, and ambitions.

The Benefits of Being Rooted in Creativity

Constructive, confrontational creativity gives us the opportunity to show and share what we believe in. Many heated discussions ensue when people find themselves committed to opposite sides of a cause or a client's project. Creatively resolving these confrontational moments builds trust and relationships with team members. Creativity lets us take a stand, ask questions, express our thoughts, and be open to debate while respecting others. It's an efficient way of working in today's overfull world.

L'Oréal has a space called "the confrontation room," where employees confront ideas. Despite being a large and established company, L'Oréal is known for its innovation. It's no coincidence that a creative company that values confrontation has achieved global market dominance. L'Oréal uses that approach when choosing what to launch or how to innovate skin cream, shampoo, and other widely used products. Creativity springs from fierce, confrontational debate. When we provided training for L'Oréal, young product managers entered the ring with the marketing director to come up with the best course of action for resolving conflict and keeping projects in motion.

You probably use creativity every day without knowing it. When we think on our feet and adapt spontaneously, we build our creative mind. Logistics and organizational changes require a creative mentality. Even the process of adjusting and readjusting to health restrictions and changing regulations requires a tremendous amount of creativity.

The creative capacity in my company lets us design programs that push people to work on their creativity and assertiveness. I often receive positive feedback from companies that were once stuck in their approach to a project because our consulting helped them find an amicable and profitable solution. Our clients benefit greatly from this process that inherently generates and iterates many ideas in a short amount of time. That capacity offers a competitive advantage and keeps organizations moving forward.

If we want to dance with chaos, creativity is imperative. Working in a complex work environment or on complex projects requires the ability to make spontaneous changes and help others do the same.

In order to stay rooted, we need to recognize our natural creativity and realize that Herbert Spencer's philosophy of survival of the fittest may indeed be survival of the most creative. We can use creativity to bring hope, inspire courage, maintain focus, and build relationships. But when our approach to creativity matches the speed of this fast-paced world, we will be ready to dance.

Genie™ Prompts for Creativity

Go to www.talk2genie.com and type in one of these conversation starters:

- Help me brainstorm new ideas for something
- Let's create a daily creativity routine
- I want to overcome creative blocks
- Create a mind map for a project
- Build a creative workspace
- Let's enhance my creative thinking skills
- I want to collaborate on a creative project

Practical Tips to up your game with CREATIVITY.

Make it real, keep it simple, you're a rock star ☺

These creativity-based tools and techniques can be powerful aids in enhancing your creative thinking and problem-solving abilities in an ever-shifting, accelerating world. You can choose the ones that resonate most with your personal style and adapt them to your creative process.

Reverse Brainstorm:
One really helpful and fun creativity technique is the Reverse Brainstorm tool: Take an objective like "We want to finish the project on time" and reverse it, "We want to finish the project late." Set a timer for 2 minutes and make the longest list possible of ways to finish late. Then turn off the timer and look at how you can re-engineer your ways back to finishing on time. It's a lot of fun and really works well!

Six Thinking Hats (Edward de Bono):
Use the Six Thinking Hats method to approach a problem or idea from six different perspectives, each represented by a different colored "hat." For example, the white hat represents facts and information, the red hat represents emotions and feelings, and so on. This technique encourages holistic thinking and helps generate creative solutions by considering various viewpoints.

The Dreamer, The Critic and the Realist (Walt Disney):
Adopt Walt Disney's creative strategy, which involves three distinct roles: the Dreamer, the Realist, and the Critic. When working on a project or idea, start with the Dreamer phase to generate wild, imaginative ideas. Then switch to the Realist phase to plan and outline the practical steps needed. Finally, enter the Critic phase to evaluate and refine the concept. This structured approach balances creativity with practicality.

6

Practice

Watching a dance troupe move in a synchronous fluid motion may be one of the most beautiful and awe-inspiring performances you'll ever see. Even the timing of gloved hand dancers leaves us stunned. Few realize the hours that go into such remarkable displays.

The hip-hop dancers at the Superbowl practice at least seventy-two hours over nine days for their twenty-six-minute presentation, and all over the world each fall corps de ballet begin rehearsing six hours every day to be ready for "Nutcracker" season. Even those professionals who've danced the Tchaikovsky classic for years participate in the grueling rehearsals.

Acting taught me great lessons in deliberate, disciplined practice. Learning lines, using effective voice techniques, and employing Meisner's principles of emotional preparation, repetition, and improvisation only touch the surface of everything required of theater hopefuls. Rehearsal—on your own and with the troupe provides the only means to a successful night on the stage.

I believe everyone should take at least one acting class. The craft hones a core of deeply essential skills, like listening, repetition, and muscle memorization. Live theater emulates today's changing world because it involves intense practice to bring shows to the public and quickly adapt when someone forgets a line or a prop doesn't work as planned. With proper practice, repeat patrons rarely notice that no two performances are exactly alike.

Being surrounded by other actors at Northwestern University and receiving support from inspiring instructors changed my life. The expectation of commitment was so high that we knew not to show up to class without knowing our lines, emotions, and places. Each participant arrived on time, ready to work. Those who lacked full commitment found themselves dropped from the program, so we went all in.

I truly admire my acting friends, both pre- and post-Northwestern. Many kept up the intense schedule, and after a decade of constant practice, multiple rejections, and financial worry, they went on to become well known and successful in their careers. Like most musicians, dancers, and actors, they also held down a second or third job to pay the bills, ignoring the long hours and the fact they were grossly overqualified.

That degree of commitment and discipline is remarkable, but leaders in every industry will tell you that you can't gain mastery without putting in the time and practice.

Repetition Creates Expertise

Even the most naturally talented can't master their gift if they only do it once in a while. And this practice is not limited to the arts or sports. If we want to shape our behavior and mindset, we need to practice just as diligently. Building new habits requires repeating the action until it becomes natural.

Writing is an iterative process that requires constant refinement. No book would be ready for publishing after completion of the first draft. Stephen King said writers must be prepared to cut twenty-five percent of everything they write. Disciplined authors reread, rewrite, and cut until they find the polished manuscript worthy of print.

J.K. Rowling proved this theory when she published the second book in the Harry Potter Series without revisions. She thought it could ride the coattails of the first. As a result, the second is considered by many to be the worst in the series.

In the current culture, people who have unique, highly developed skills stand out. And achieving those mastery levels means pushing ourselves out of our comfort zones into something bigger and bolder than what others around us are doing.

With the time constraints of the modern world, we try to squeeze many things into our day. So we have to use the rooting tool of focus to narrow down our list. Focus and practice go hand in hand. Both require discipline and as we narrow our focus, we'll find more time for the repetition required to reach our goals.

By homing in on our why, we can prioritize the things that are most important to us. These are the things we practice. Even if we fail at the beginning, we have to keep going. It's tempting to say we tried it, it didn't work out, and quit. And even if you push ahead, you may not notice improvement right away. Some will see incremental change, and others will practice a long time, and suddenly that thing you thought you'd never be able to do becomes possible. Giving up too soon would be a shame.

In addition to helping mold our thinking, practice aids in developing methods or systems. Repetition will mean we can eventually perform the task without notes. Choreography becomes part of a dancer's being the more she practices. Guitar players find the next chord with ease. Muscle memory completes the action without much thought. When we rehearse our speech as if it's important to us, we can deliver the message without looking at our notes.

The beauty of this kind of repetitive practice, regardless of how boring it seems or how much precious time it takes, is the confidence level it builds. Anxiety levels drop and you feel better about yourself and your performance.

Invest in Your Craft

All over the world, parents with children as young as two are paying dance instructors to help them learn the basics of the art. Even the most naturally gifted musicians and artists will pay a master to help them to refine their craft.

When I started my consulting business, I thought I could find clients by simply introducing myself and offering my service. I quickly realized I needed help. So, I invested the little money I had in virtual coaching sessions. I still use those lessons on a daily basis. I've practiced them so often they've become ingrained in my thinking and behavior.

My dialectic training taught me a great deal about negotiation; however, I still invested time practicing, learning, and ingesting other schools of arbitration. Ultimately, the time and money I invested made me feel good about my new career path. Starting and running a business requires a level of commitment that resonates with the practice of my theater days.

Committing to practice and investing time and money in your craft also bring the reward of self-perpetuating motivation. The more you practice the easier it becomes, it's a virtuous circle. In fact, it's possible to get hooked on practice.

Practicing a new skill doesn't have to consume your schedule. One hour can go a long way toward keeping your mind sharp and engaged. The brain is like a muscle, exercising it makes it stronger. When you stop exercising it, you lose strength. Fortunately, when you resume the exercise, the strength returns fairly quickly. For instance, a language you don't use will become lost. But once you start speaking it again, you'll be surprised what you remember. Even a daily hour of practice can have significant results for your skill mastery. And applying the same dedication to exercising your mind can help your cognitive acuity.

Practice is as Natural as Child's Play

Children practice without even realizing it. When wee ones play, they practice gross-and fine-motor skills. Play dates allow them to rehearse their social skills. From birth, they practice bonding, and each vocalization is a preparation for conversation. Every new toy encourages them to practice their adaptive and learning skills. And while they might not realize it, homework provides another opportunity for repetitive learning.

The phenomenon isn't limited to humans. When puppies bite and wrestle with the other members of their litter, they are learning, and tiger cubs play games that look like hunting.

One goal of the programs my company offers for successful executives is helping the participants see practice as a game. We often give them exercises that are funny, exaggerated, and over the top. We want them to enjoy themselves while they are being challenged to learn and refine new skills.

Those who have a hard time finding the discipline and willpower to push through practice are encouraged to ask themselves three questions.

- How can you make the practice fun for yourself?

- How can you gamify the experience?

- How can you play while you practice?

Practice develops new neural pathways in the brain, and if we can find ways to enjoy the activity, we have a better chance of making these pathways even stronger. In the first year of life, babies develop an astronomical number of pathways each day. Early development requires a great deal of mental energy which is one reason they sleep so much.

Neural pathway growth extends to adults as well. Our brains form new neural strings in response to our experiences. This happens most often in response to injury or disease, but when a person focuses their attention on any area enough, they can rewire their brain and create neural pathways. Therefore, the repetition of any practice, even negativity or positivity, can retrain and strengthen your brain. [17]

As we age, it's even more vital to engage in activities that will strengthen the brain. Aging naturally reduces the number of neural pathways; however, by working the mind, and getting adequate sleep and exercise, we can keep building. A deliberate choice to take a class or engage in practicing a new language or activity can slow cognitive decline. [18]

My mother still works as a psychologist. She doesn't need to work, but she enjoys her job. Her profession helps keep her sharp and encourages her to come up with new ideas.

Additionally, she remains socially involved. For instance, she's been part of a book club for more than twenty years. Because she practices finding innovative ideas and reading challenging books, she stimulates new neural pathways and keeps her brain young.

The Value of Practice

Practice implies imperfections and mistakes. So, sometimes it will feel like you are wasting your time. You'll buy the wrong book or pick the wrong coach. You might spend three hours working hard, only to find out the person you invested time in isn't a good fit. But it's never a waste because when we wade through what doesn't work, we learn what does.

Accept from the outset that you won't always succeed. There will be moments of failure, false starts, and dead ends. And each of those moments will contain lessons. You may find that what you learn from the bad experience is more valuable than what you lost in failing to meet your goal.

For example, sometimes my consultants struggle developing a new educational program. We may have budgeted a day for a project that takes a day and a half. Another company may fret about the extra expense or lost time. Instead of getting worked up, my team keeps the big picture in mind. Some projects simply take more or less time. And the more we practice, the less time these projects will take. But practicing without worrying what some may view as failures helps them develop their skills and do their best possible work.

I've found the most successful people don't complain about extra time they spent practicing their skills. Practice will ultimately open doors. Those with the scarcity mindset worry about those few extra minutes, while an abundance mindset values the experience as much as time and money.

Geoff Colvin wrote an amazing book called *Talent is Overrated*. He reasons that deliberate practice makes top performers stand apart from everyone else even more than talent. He references people like Bill Gates, Steve Jobs, and Michael Jordan. Colvin tells the story of a famous baseball player on his way to becoming the next Babe Ruth. His coach identified the one skill that would give him that competitive advantage. Then in a very deliberate, specific way, the coach developed a targeted, repetitive practice plan for the player. He added this extra layer to his regular training. In the movie, The Natural, Roy Hobbs' father tells him, "You've got a gift, Roy. But it's not enough. You've got to develop yourself. If you rely too much on your own gift . . . you'll fail." [19]

When a person has a high level of natural talent, they don't think they need to practice. Nevertheless, with practice they can go from a 9.9 to a 10 and edge out the competition. Deliberate practice develops precision and regularity. It separates the top from the pinnacle.

Malcolm Gladwell's book *Outliers* says in order to become an expert, you must invest 10,000 hours in your craft. Since we have limited time, we have to carefully choose how we use our time.

Taking it Public

While practicing alone makes for a great start, eventually, you need others. A dance troupe needs each member to be in sync, every instrument in the orchestra has to learn to hear the others, and actors need to practice timing and direction. Deliberate practice is never a solo venture.

The most valuable form of practice is with someone who is incredibly skilled in your field of interest—someone who can guide, demonstrate, and honestly critique. This outside perspective reveals your blind spots. We all have them. But we have to be willing to receive the feedback, even if it feels unpleasant. How will we know the areas that need more rehearsal if no one tells us which steps we're missing?

We also need to become comfortable practicing our skills in public. Pianists and dancers have recitals, middle school bands host concerts because the young people get better when they know someone is watching. Even the stage is a practice arena as the performer learns to keep going through their nerves and how to fall or make mistakes with grace.

Relationships need the same kind of platform. Connecting with others requires practice. Whether it's a business relationship, friendship, or romance, relationships require constant work. Every relationship moves like a dance if we allow it. Sometimes we lead, and other times we follow.

In a romantic relationship, we practice by dating and then partnering. This means we might have to kiss a bunch of toads along the way, but in each connection, we learn as much about ourselves as we do about relating. Learning how to best connect with others happens gradually, and the knowledge allows us to become more collaborative, form stronger relationships, and cultivate resilience. Even after years in a relationship, the connection takes work. As people grow and evolve, so will the relationship. You can't set it and forget it. Without practice, you'll have no relationship.

Editing and revisions should be done in public as well. Each time we pitch ideas and present services, we figure out how to do it better the next time. We learn to think strategically based on what we uncovered during our last public rehearsal. Every public engagement becomes a stepping stone toward your best self.

For nearly two decades, I've been creating formal presentations that we use in the final round of our RFP proposals. These in-person pitches require large amounts of energy and mental focus. They used to drain me. However, I learned to look at each one as a practice field. Afterwards, I could compare proposals I'd lost with the ones I'd won and determine which areas of my presentation needed more practice outside of the public eye. Ultimately, this led to less nerves over time because I became rooted in my ability—an ability I polished through practice.

Even with my added confidence, I continue to analyze each presentation with my team so we can keep up with the ever-changing landscape. We look at why we won or lost the last ten to twenty proposals. How can we refine, adapt, and innovate our process—what can we, or should we, change?

Practice keeps us fresh and allows us to keep up with the tempo of the exponential curve. Constantly evaluating what we need to rehearse and listening to the more skilled as they point out areas that could use practice builds confidence and helps root us. Practice works well to build hope and courage, which encourages us to practice even more. Practice increases our focus, and when we work with others to sharpen our skills, we develop strong, trustworthy relationships. And perhaps more than anything else, practice gives us the freedom to release our creativity. These six practices root us as the world spins out of control. Learning these rooting principles gives us the foundational steps so as we accelerate, we can begin our dance with chaos.

Genie™ Prompts for Practice

Go to www.talk2genie.com and type in one of these conversation starters:

- Help me build a consistent practice routine
- Let's create a practice plan for my skill
- I want to overcome obstacles in my practice
- Create a system for tracking my practice progress
- Build a habit of regular reflection on my practice
- Let's enhance my practice efficiency
- I want to integrate new skills into my practice routine

Practical Tips to up your game with PRACTICE.

Make it real, keep it simple, you're a rock star ☺

These exercises are designed to help you incrementally enhance your skills and expertise and adapt to the ever-changing demands of a fast-moving and complex world. By dedicating consistent effort, seeking feedback, and using deliberate practice strategies, you can make significant progress and adapt your skills to changing circumstances.

Microlearning Sessions:
Break down your skill development into short, focused, and frequent microlearning sessions. Allocate just 2-5 minutes (super short sequence) or 5-15 minutes (short sequence) each day to practice and improve a specific skill. Whether it's learning a new language, mastering a musical instrument, or enhancing your coding abilities, consistent, bite-sized practice can work the new skill into your system and general habit pool and over time will yield significant results.

Feedback Loops:
Create a feedback loop for your skill development. Seek feedback from mentors or peers or self-assess your progress regularly. Constructive feedback helps you identify areas for improvement and adjust your practice techniques accordingly. Embrace the feedback as an opportunity to refine your skills. Sometimes it helps to think of feedback as a gift you are receiving or giving if the situation is reversed.

Deliberate Practice:
Implement deliberate practice techniques for skill enhancement. This involves setting specific, challenging goals, breaking them down into smaller tasks, and practicing with a high level of focus and intention. For example, if you're a writer, set a goal to write a certain number of words per day, study the craft of storytelling, and analyze your writing critically for improvement.

In a business context, deliberate practice could involve a salesperson rehearsing and refining their sales pitch, addressing objections, and seeking feedback from mentors or colleagues. They might repeatedly practice specific elements of the pitch to enhance their overall effectiveness and adaptability in sales situations.

PART TWO

Discovering Acceleration Skills

7

Adaptability

Getting yourself rooted is imperative if you want to be able to dance in this fast-paced ever-changing environment. But to survive, we need to find a way to keep up, and that means learning to accelerate at the same speed or faster than the exponentially evolving culture. The trick is to increase speed without falling into the trap of expending more energy—a snare that many of us fall into. Yes, we'll find instances when moving slowly and deliberately serves us well, but those who can accelerate, dancing in sync with the rhythm of change instead of letting the noise of the world steal their momentum, ultimately succeed.

Dancing with Adaptability

Improvised and impromptu offerings have been a part of music for centuries. The theater added them in the first millennium. Dance Improv has slowly made its way into the craft in the last four hundred years. Every performing art and successful business have started to realize the value of taking the rooting traits and using them to adapt.

Performers who work together to create something never seen before in front of an audience have spent hours learning how to adapt to every situation. By honing their skills, they can anticipate the moves of the other performers, allowing each musician and dancer to quickly add their unique talent to make the stage come alive.

Adaptability develops like a muscle; it needs practice and exercise. Recent studies from McKinsey, the World Economic Forum, and Boston Consulting Group, among others, repeatedly rank adaptability among the top five most sought-after skills in professional environments. The concept of adaptability could fill ten volumes on its own and relates to every other concept in this book. Adaptability is the child of creativity and practice. It gives birth to hope and requires courage.

Survival of the Adaptable

Nature constantly proves the value of adaptability. Darwin's study of the peppered moth offers one of the most obvious demonstrations. The scientist noted that the black spotted white moths changed over time in order to survive. When the industrial age deteriorated the air quality and killed the lichen on the trees, the moths underwent a genetic mutation that caused them to be dark. They had to either adapt to their surroundings or be eaten by the birds. One hundred years later, pollution controls brought the lichen back, as well as the light-colored moths. These quickly adapting insects proved Darwin's thoughts. "It is not the strongest of the species that survives nor the most intelligent that survives. It's the one that is the most adaptable to change." Sometimes adaptability makes the difference between floundering and succeeding, and other times it truly determines whether we survive or die.

The world learned the importance of adaptability in the aftermath of the attack on the towers in New York City and other notable landmarks in the United States. Canceled flights and the uncertainty of travel ramped up security in airports around the globe. Likewise, the pandemic of 2020 forced nations to adapt. Lockdowns took people from living and moving about freely to complying with severe restrictions. Parents adapted by learning how to home school, bedrooms were adapted to create home offices, and non-necessary service industries and their staff members had to find creative adaptations to keep their heads above water. In France, we found ourselves confined to our apartments for two and a half months, adapting to one hour or less outside each day. Adaptation became the only choice for the entire world. Our willingness to adapt—or lack thereof—will shape our future.

Professional Adaptability

Every human and most animals are born with an innate sense of adaptability. With the exponential rate of change we face in the twenty-first century, a turbo-charged version of adaptability is imperative.

My company adapts our offering regularly. The market shifts around 2015 began to make our approach obsolete. At the same time, because of the way it affected various industries, we didn't have to work as hard to persuade executives the importance of soft skill training; clients sought us out.

As the speed of change accelerated, our ability to adapt also accelerated. In 2016, we began experimenting with a variety of formats and took more risks in our highly action-oriented approach. We were able to take those risks because our clients were changing faster, too. We all won as a result, going further together than ever before.

By 2019, the industry had turned to digitized skill building, but I found the mainstream approach horribly boring—people watching animated slides about giving effective feedback or persuading a steering committee. My team became inspired to develop an innovative method and platform for building soft skills with an action- and emotion-based digital approach. We use experimentation and practice, and coaches connect deeply with participants to encourage vulnerability and risk-taking.

When COVID hit, we had to adapt again. All of our signature in person training programs needed to be virtualized. We started with dozens of tailor-made programs and worked up to hundreds. Had we not adjusted, we would have folded. What I missed most was the face-to-face interactions. I value the emotional energy and the way every gesture and facial expression heightens interaction. At first, it was difficult to recreate that kind of energy via videoconference, but we practiced until it felt more natural. We examined the source of that vibration in person and figured out how to achieve the same effects virtually. The pandemic provided a catalyst to forming a new set of approaches.

Some of my coaches weren't able to adjust to the new working environment. Others created a massive amount of energy, desire, commitment, curiosity, and connection in the virtual setting. We debriefed, brainstormed alternatives, and collaborated as a team to iterate and improve.

Despite the turmoil around us, we experienced twenty-two percent growth in 2020 and seventy percent growth in 2021.

Our team quickly adapting to a hands-on, action focused virtual approach was essential to our surviving and thriving.

Increasing Your Adaptability Quotient

Everyone has heard of an Intelligent Quotient (IQ), and the world has started to recognize the Emotional Quotient (EQ). Now businesses are beginning to talk about the Adaptability Quotient (AQ), and as time passes, AQ will become more and more important. Whether you're applying for an entry-level job or a more strategic, high-level career, adaptability is an indispensable skill for success. Those who fail to adapt to the changing workplace will not thrive.

Some people are born to be adaptable, but anyone can increase their ability to adapt. With each experience and environment, we can practice adapting. Every challenge, every success, and even your failures can shape you.

People have the power to change significantly, much more than they think. We all have the capacity to increase our AQ, but our level of progress is directly related to our willingness to learn. Every kind of challenge can be a learning experience—divorce, loss of a loved one, business evolution, economic restructuring, and more present opportunities for us to practice adaptability.

In addition, our environment largely influences our ability to adapt. By surrounding ourselves with supportive people and monitoring our stress, we increase our adaptability. A strong support system allows us to be more open and relaxed. We feel more comfortable with experimenting and voicing our opinion allowing us to practice our adaptability.

And while zero stress is impossible, and excessive stress strains your nervous system, physiology, emotions, and cognitive capacities, without any challenges, we will actually become less adaptable. But between the extremes is a sweet spot of stress that is stimulating and motivating at a level that matches our resources, capabilities, and objectives in a healthy way. There is a level of stress that can facilitate our adaptability quotient.

Adapting to a Digital Society

The science of AQ is an emerging field, but substantial data already exists to quantitatively describe adaptability. Despite the explosive growth in interest in the subject, many leaders remain skeptical.

Humans have been adapting since the beginning of time. The stone age, the bronze age, and the iron age were all adaptations. But the adaptations began increasing exponentially when the world entered the industrial revolution. From coal to gas, to electronics and renewable energy, humanity has progressed faster than our ancestors ever imagined. Now, in the midst of the digital revolution, businesses have to adapt to meet the needs of humankind. Everything is changing—the way we work, make food, practice medicine, and so much more. People have dreams of creating an interplanetary species, and we have to learn to interface with artificial intelligence. Our choices are adapt or become increasingly disconnected.

One of the unintended results of the digital revolution is that people have become more and more isolated. Instead of grabbing a coffee with friends, we send a text apologizing for being too busy. With the move to social media, many relationships have become superficial, and it's often easier to unfriend or block someone than work on creating community. Fewer in-person interactions means that despite the means to become more and more connected, our society has become increasingly detached.

This age of change calls us to find new ways to meet our need for human associations. Intellectually, we might think we're sufficiently connected because of the number of "friends" we have on Facebook or contacts on LinkedIn. We exchange texts with real friends and have occasional group meals with colleagues. Every day, we see an endless stream of faces on Zoom or Teams. However, it's important not to confuse those passing exchanges with true, deep, and meaningful connections. Adapting to the digital age without leaving personal connections behind is essential.

My teams help people connect more consciously with others, their meaning, their mission, their work, and with who they are. As the world continues to evolve and accelerate, we'll see creative initiatives to facilitate this. It is paradoxically easier and harder than ever to connect in the digital age—easy on a superficial level and extremely challenging on a deeper level.

The exponential speed of change presents a challenge. If everyone doesn't up their AQ, society will split into tiers of those who have adapted and those who have not. Soon, we'll have the technology to automate more and more roles. Plus, fewer people want traditional occupations like basic administrative, office, and service jobs. With those positions harder and harder to fill, automation becomes an even more plausible solution.

What will happen to those who, for whatever reason, don't grasp the importance of adaptability? They'll be left behind. So, those who've learned to adapt have a responsibility to encourage and assist the people around them as they find their place in the digital world.

It's amazing how many people—even young, working people—are not adapting to the digital age and improving their skills with technology. Some even avoid email and texts.

How will they function in the future as digital communication becomes even more sophisticated?

How has your life changed in the past five years? Workplace environments evolved at an accelerated pace during that time. It has become increasingly common to work remotely and never meet coworkers in real life. Not that long ago, video conferencing, VPNs, and other remote technology began to make its way into business. Still, it was culturally unacceptable to untether entirely from physical offices. Becoming a digital nomad, a person who moves from location to location but reliably collaborates with a consistent team has become a popular profession. The pandemic accelerated the shift to remote and flexible work schedule.

A person with a high AQ doesn't need an office to be productive. Some find themselves even more useful in a variety of changing environments. In the past, working outside an office gave the impression of someone less committed or productive. Now, though, digital nomadism projects a more accurate image—one that puts an emphasis on core competence over performative work and demonstrates high adaptability.

The ACE Model

My company has partnered with an organization called AQai to use an assessment they developed to measure and address the Adaptability Quotient within an organization.

Our shared mission is to co-elevate and help people find greater well-being and performance through better adaptability. We seek to help people understand how the speed and scope of the change we're experiencing necessitates the acceleration of adaptability skills.

AQai's assessment, the ACE model, measures fifteen different sub skills of adaptability in the areas of Ability,

Character, and Environment. Technology Advancements are driving down the need for hard skills. Even during the months of my writing this book, artificial intelligence and the way people use it has changed exponentially. The ACE assessment can help us determine the areas that might resist such drastic change and show us how to build our adaptability quotient.

The first dimension of the ACE model is Ability. Its five sub skills include Unlearn, Mental Flexibility, Grit, Mindset, and Resilience. All these subskills are improvable and highly coachable. Those who want to keep ahead of the exponential curve know they need to learn new skills; however, they will also have to develop a capacity to unlearn. In order to effectively adapt, we must be willing and able to learn quickly, while letting go of old ways and thoughts. This openness to new ideas leads to mental flexibility and helps us develop the grit needed to forge ahead.

Cultivating a positive outlook on change and seeing the glass as half-full enables us to shape the mindset needed to thrive in today's world. This mental filter identifies opportunities instead of obstacles and creates resilience.

These skills may not cause each other—grit doesn't necessarily increase your ability to unlearn—but they are highly correlated.

The second dimension is character. These sub skills relate to an individual's innate personality; however, each is more malleable than most imagine, though not as extensively as the ability subskills. With increased awareness and coaching, we can develop Extroversion, Hope, Motivational style, Thinking style, and Emotional response.

Because these five are very personality driven, one characteristic might be easier to develop than another. One of the wonderful things about adaptability is that you don't have to reinforce every subskill to increase your overall AQ. You can increase your strengths or focus on one or two weaknesses. Every improvement raises your adaptability level.

An introverted person may need to push themselves to meet new people or embark on new endeavors. However, if you do not feel inclined to be more extroverted, you could focus on your motivational style. Some are motivated by winning, others by protecting. People with a play to win motivational style tend to be more adaptable. Growth drives them. They play from an abundance mindset—there is plenty available, I just have to figure out how to get my share. On the other hand, play to protect styles think more along the lines of scarcity—supplies are limited, we must protect what we have at all costs. To become adaptable, those who feel a need to protect the current status can develop character by playing to win and looking for ways to grow the next time they face a challenge, try to close a sale, or work to get a project approved.

The final dimension is environment. This includes your Work support, Work stress, Company support, Team support, and Emotional health.

Much of our environment dimension is based on perception, and that perception makes us more or less adaptable. Managers and leaders have a powerful arsenal of practices and initiatives they can put into place to raise their team's adaptability. Fostering a supportive environment where different team members can voice their ideas, share setbacks and difficulties, and propose new solutions without fearing mean-spirited criticism or other retribution will naturally augment the overall AQ of the group.

Thanks to AQai's assessment, it's possible to take your individual AQ measurement. A delightful AI named Aida asks a series of questions that produces a report summarizing the level of each subskill. If you discover your unlearn level is very high but your grit level is quite low, you can use that information to decide how to best use your subskills. For example, would increasing your grit help in your current context? Since you're good at unlearning, what old knowledge should you abandon to best serve the current situation?

Adaptability as a scientific concept isn't new, but the ACE model is on the cutting edge of adaptability research. It helps us develop an awareness of our ability to adapt to technological change and consciously cultivate that adaptability in a meaningful, day-to-day way.

Mindset Check

There are a few questions we can ask to determine the baseline of our adaptability quotient:

- Are you open to evolving and accepting new things, or does change bring tension as you assume your situation will be worse than it was before?

- Do you focus on the current shortfalls of new technology, or do you see the potential?

- Do you let your technological ignorance block learning and make you self-conscious, or are you okay looking foolish while doing something for the first time because it's just so cool to be trying it?

Our reactions to change significantly impact our outcomes. For example, like it or not, the ever advancing technology will change the current landscape of our meetings. The approaches we use today will phase out, and something new will rise to the forefront. Think about the evolution of phones. In less than one hundred fifty years, landlines moved from their first use to almost obsolete, simple cellular devices used only by businesses became a handheld computer in every person's back pocket in just three decades.

Everything technology related is destined to follow the same pattern. If you don't adapt, you won't even be a part of it. I share AQai's goal to leave no one behind. It's important for me to help raise consciousness of adaptability and its indispensability in the current age, so as many people as possible can exist comfortably, not just in the world of today but also the world of tomorrow. A quick web search of pages dated only a few years ago reveal technology predictions that appeared well before anticipated. Without a mindset of adaptability, we won't be able to keep up. This is why my company has developed cutting edge programs to teach and practice these crucial skills linked to adaptability.

Each season, even the youngest dancers learn new choreography. They build on skills they learned the year before and discard the moves they've outgrown. Their ability to adapt to the new rhythms and steps allows them to create beauty and intrigue. Similarly, when we are conscious of the importance of adaptability and choose to develop its dimensions, we have a much greater chance of accelerating our progress. When we learn the most recent chaotic dance, we lose feelings of being overwhelmed and are better able to keep up with the quickly-changing world.

Genie™ Prompts for Adaptability

Go to www.talk2genie.com and type in one of these conversation starters:

- Help me become more adaptable in my work
- Let's create a plan to handle unexpected changes
- I want to improve my resilience to setbacks
- Create a routine to enhance my adaptability skills
- Build a mindset for embracing change

- Let's enhance my ability to learn new skills quickly
- Develop strategies for staying flexible under pressure

Practical Tips to up your game with ADAPTABILITY.

Make it real, keep it simple, you're a rock star ☺

These practical exercises help to boost your adaptability in the face of constant and intense change. They can help you develop the psychological and emotional resilience needed to thrive in a fast-moving and complex world and become more adaptable in your personal and professional life.

Daily Routine Change-Up:
Embrace adaptability by deliberately altering elements of your daily routine. Begin with small changes like changing your morning rituals, trying a new route to work, or rearranging your workspace. Observe how you adapt and what insights you gain. Gradually introduce more significant changes, such as taking on new responsibilities at work or exploring a new hobby. This progressive approach helps you build a resilient mindset, making you better prepared for larger transitions in the future.

"What If" Scenario Challenge:
Regularly challenge yourself with "What If" scenarios related to your work or life. Ask questions like, "What if a major project gets delayed?" or "What if I have to change my career direction?" or "What if I need to change my child's school?" Then, brainstorm practical solutions and contingency plans. This exercise encourages you to think on your feet, adapt to unforeseen circumstances, and become more comfortable

with change by preparing for various outcomes. Your confidence in adapting to constant and intense change will soar!

Adaptability Feedback Rounds:
Implement regular "Adaptability Feedback Rounds" during team meetings or project debriefs. Encourage team members to openly share their experiences with experimentation and any associated failures. Emphasize the value of learning from setbacks and applying those lessons to improve team performance and communication. Create a safe, non-judgmental space for team members to discuss their experiences. This will help foster a culture of openness to failure as an essential component of adaptability.

8

Confidence

During my first pregnancy, I frequently searched BabyCenter for different signs and symptoms to see if my progress was normal. If I didn't feel the baby move for even half an hour, I'd worry. Some baby book told me if you don't feel the baby moving and want reassurance, you should drink a glass of orange juice and lie down. The sugar reaches the baby pretty quickly and causes them to stir. Nearly every day, I drank orange juice and waited for the baby to move.

I don't even like orange juice.

After the first trimester of my second pregnancy, when statistically most dangers have passed, I searched for information a handful of times. My previous experience had elevated my confidence, and nearly eliminated doubt and worry.

My friends demonstrate the same pattern. One evening, as I put my daughter into her pajamas, the two-month-old kept getting her finger caught in her sleeve. I joked to my friend, mother of three children, standing nearby, "I must have forgotten how to put on pajamas since the last one." She laughed. "By the third baby, you don't even put them in pajamas."

Another friend who has three children said that during her first pregnancy, she spent ten hours just shopping for the best thermometer to check the bathwater temperature. With each bath, if the water wasn't within half a degree of ideal, she'd rerun the water. For baby number two, she checked the water with her hand. For the third one, she quipped, "You put the baby in. If they don't cry, it's the right temperature." That's confidence.

Confidence gives us energy, strength, and courage to go boldly toward what we want. Otherwise, we flounder or fail to take action.

In today's chaotic world, we need to be able to take in and process information quickly, often to make time-sensitive decisions. Without confidence, you hesitate or choose the safest option. These decisions may not advance you toward your goals. You may find more obstacles in your way.

It's tempting to brush past the issue of confidence. But even in the midst of our busy lives, it's important to stop and consider the messages we send ourselves. While some are quite aware they don't have the level of self-confidence they would like, others have a superficial confidence, or they feel confident about what they produce but not about themselves.

Growing Confidence Beyond Our Comfort Zones

Some people's high levels of confidence are limited to their comfort zone. But in this accelerating world, we need to tackle new tasks, problems, questions, and projects outside our comfort zones all the time. With everything changing at an increasingly dizzying rate, we need confidence in ourselves to go beyond the familiar.

Are you fully confident in your ability to explore areas outside your comfort zone? In considering how to approach new situations and goals, Dan Sullivan came up with a wonderful four-step process called The 4 C's Formula®: Commitment leads to courage which develops competence and creates confidence. As we gain confidence, we are more able to commit to the next foreign idea or project. Those four C's perfectly illustrate the need to find courage when you make a commitment. Dan tells us that courage is the most difficult part.

This is why we should always be working to grow our confidence—it's not a static trait. You need new confidence each time you face an unfamiliar challenge, project, objective, or goal. Success in this exponentially expanding world requires committing to the task with courage, and confidence comes from faking it until you make it and following through.

Confidence serves as an accelerating factor because it allows you to go faster sooner. You give up wavering between choices. It doesn't mean you never make mistakes. On the other hand, it gives you permission to make them. Confidence understands that mistakes are inevitable, and most aren't catastrophic. We speed up our learning curve when we have confidence in our overall resilience and ability.

I've learned that it doesn't matter if I hit an obstacle. I trust I'll figure it out and do better next time. Confidence developed over time allows me to be imperfect in front of people I admire. I'm mastering the art of proceeding at the risk of looking foolish. Worst-case scenario is I'll embarrass myself. Whether I do or not, I'll move on. Confidence that comes through trial and error pushes me outside my comfort zone and gives me an edge as I deal with the world.

Confidence in Self

Confidence has three facets. Confidence in yourself, confidence in others, and confidence in the larger world. Having confidence in yourself has an enormous effect on how you react to events as well as how you filter and make decisions.

Consider having a meeting with the CEO of a company. A lack of confidence will make you doubt yourself. Who am I to ask for this person's time? As a result, you might never take a step to make it happen. If you do set up the meeting, that same doubt will keep you from entering with the sense of authority needed to start the relationship on the right footing.

By contrast, if you fully believe in yourself, you'll find creative flow. You will take bold and audacious actions to reach your goals. So many dreams die because people don't believe in themselves.

Self-confidence is believing at a deep level that you are worthy. Humans struggle with questions of worthiness to some extent throughout life. We all have moments of more or less confidence. However, we must take care not to fall into pits of doubt. The confident accept themselves. They trust that they will ultimately reach their goals or find other goals to pursue.

Such confidence doesn't mean you will always feel fully secure—it's human to have insecurities, even at high levels of success. No one gets it right every time. Confidence that doesn't acknowledge the possibility of failure is arrogance. However, deep-rooted confidence puts wind in your sails.

It's part of the human experience to carry wounds from past experiences. Not all come from ill intentions on the part of others, still those scars can lead to limiting beliefs about what we're worth, what we're capable of, and what is possible. Even when we think we've moved beyond the hurt, sometimes they creep back in. As a result, we continually have opportunities to reexamine and cultivate confidence, self-esteem, and healthier beliefs—to change ourselves and our outlook over time. Such self-work has always been important but is particularly vital if we want to achieve our goals amid the chaos, complexity, and speed of the current world.

Confidence in Others

Confidence in others represents a powerful acceleration factor. When people get suspicious or skeptical because of past disappointment, that painful memory can become ingrained. Doubt and distrust cloud their lens and blind them to new opportunities.

Whether or not you approach others with confidence will shape your interactions and determine how you interpret what they say or propose. I'm not advocating unearned trust—actions speak louder than words. If you cannot have confidence in the people you work with because of their actions, then you need to work with different people. If you have grounds to lack confidence in your friends, then it's time to seek a new circle.

Repeated bad actions should be a red flag, but when you enter a new situation, it is better to start with a general confidence in others' good intentions. If you default to skepticism, you'll misinterpret people acting in good faith and miss working with great staff.

Often, people don't share your ways of acting and communicating. Fortunately, they can still make excellent partners in collaboration. If you start with a climate of trust, it allows everyone involved to move forward quickly with confidence. Plus, you'll develop the ability to identify more opportunities.

Confidence in yourself and confidence in others are linked. If you're confident in yourself and your adaptability, you're more likely to begin relationships with a level of trust. Those two forces together allow you to navigate the chaotic world with a greater sense of ease. If you don't trust yourself, it's hard to trust others.

Confidence in the World

Many people describe confidence in the world as developing a mindset of abundance—you learn to see the best in opportunities. In order to see the best, we have to look for the best. It's like buying a new red car. Suddenly, you see red cars everywhere or you begin to notice that make and model. It's not that more people began driving that kind of car the same day you did, you notice it because you're inadvertently looking for it.

We all have different values, so what you focus on will depend on what's most important to you. What fills you with happiness, joy, satisfaction, and energy? There are so many demands on us today that we need to feed ourselves with pursuits that increase our energy rather than sap it.

To leverage the accelerating force of confidence and keep the wind in your sails, it's essential to view the world through a positive lens. Otherwise, you'll only see the chaos.

How to Build Confidence

The Request for Proposal processes my company engages in are long and complex, involving multiple stakeholders. When we get chosen to be a finalist in such a process, it typically concludes with a final presentation for all the stakeholders to see the service provider face to face.

Fifteen years ago, when we started making these proposals, I worried about making a mistake or someone asking a question I couldn't answer, undermining my credibility and legitimacy. That practice I mentioned earlier not only made my company better, it also increased my confidence. Though the insecurity and stress didn't entirely go away, they dramatically lessened. Nerves still surface because I care and want to win, and some adrenaline is involved. But I no longer spend sleepless nights before delivering a presentation. That foundation of confidence allows me to focus on explaining how we've thought about the client's problem and how we can solve it.

Positive-Oriented Questions

One technique my team uses to build confidence, which I find extraordinarily valuable, is asking positive-oriented questions. Most don't realize how many questions we silently ask every day in our head. Should I have another cup of coffee? Do I have time to check emails before my next meeting?

The human brain is wired to ask and answer questions. Your brain will automatically point you in the right direction when you start asking the right questions. If you feel nervous about going into a meeting, try asking yourself positive-oriented questions: Why am I feeling so good in this situation? Why am I feeling so happy to be in this situation? Why am I feeling so confident in this situation? What do I have to contribute to this meeting? Your brain will start to look for those answers.

Everyone faces negative self-talk to some degree, but we have more control over our inner monologue than we realize. If we fixate on hoping we don't screw up a presentation, whether we're wearing the right shoes, what will happen if we're late, or whether the person will like us, then our brain will amplify the negativity. On the other hand, if we orient our brain to look for the positive with a forward-moving question, we'll move toward solutions and achievement.

Positive-oriented questions offer a concrete, pragmatic way to start cutting through limiting beliefs and build self-confidence, trust in others, and faith in the world. Try questions like: In what ways is the world better off today than it was ten years ago? What amazing things happened in the world today? Those questions force an answer that will shape a positive mindset. Both the positive and the negative are true; the positive questions will not eliminate the problems, but they can help you see solutions and marshal your energy instead of engaging in cynicism and despair. If you want to fix big problems or achieve big goals, you must be in a positive lane. Otherwise, you'll hamper your own progress.

Attract Confident People

No one wants to be a Debbie Downer, and fewer want to be around her. Venting and getting worries off your chest is human and healthy, but there is a time and a place. And giving Debbie a permanent place in your thoughts will prevent you from attracting the kind of people who help you build success.

To attract others with energy you can feed off of, we must make sure we're cultivating the positive, open, confident part of our minds. We move in this direction through simple, easy methods like smiling more often and complaining less.

Promise yourself you won't complain for twenty-four hours. See how you feel, and when you're done, try it again. You'll likely feel more confident, and people will respond favorably to you and your positive, secure energy.

If you demonstrate positivity, confidence, and openness, people with those constructive qualities will want to work with you. On the other hand, if you are negative and lack confidence, you will attract people who reinforce your cynicism and self-limiting beliefs.

By becoming a person who attracts positivity, you will also recognize people who miss that groove and avoid entering dysfunctional relationships. You don't need to be happy and secure all the time, nor is it reasonable to expect it of others. Humans experience the full range of emotions. Regardless, you can cultivate a general state of peace and attract others with that mindset.

Listen to Others

Building confidence with other people has roots in understanding how to listen and take others' viewpoints into consideration. Particularly in high-stakes conversations, it's easy to take everything personally or assume people want to thwart, deceive, or defraud you.

When we stop and listen fully, we can often see their worries and motivations. And by going beyond surface level, we can better connect and feel confident in people's intentions and capacities.

My company works with many assessment tools and personality tests. We find the major breakthroughs come not from a specific tool but rather the general understanding that everyone has a different perspective. People learn, react, manage stress, and find motivation differently. Once we understand everyone is wired uniquely, we can see people in a more expansive, positive, and confidence-building way. As I discussed in the Strong Relationships chapter, connections are essential. Connection through understanding differences and giving the benefit of the doubt lets us cultivate confidence in the other person's way of doing things.

It's vital to stop talking and listen to what the person tells you. You'll understand how their minds work and discover what they see as important. That clarity will allow you to have confidence in their approach and intentions. Or if the collaboration is not a good match, you'll have the necessary information to act accordingly.

Remembering bad interactions is easy, because of the way our brains are wired for survival. We want to avoid repeating negative experiences. And though it is important not to repetitively expose ourselves to the same sources of wounds, we can also take a more expansive, nuanced approach and look for positive experiences to repeat. When we approach interactions with the intention to listen and honor differences instead of guarding ourselves and being suspicious, we'll develop confidence in more people than we ever imagined.

Reframe Your Thinking and Reconsider Your Circle

Building confidence in the world also comes down to creating a positive mindset and mental filter. Henry Ford said, "Whether you think you can, or you think you can't, you're right." He reminds us that we control a lot of our own failures and successes. Instead of succumbing to negativity, whether business or personal, list ten factors you feel confident about. Intentionally go through that exercise of identifying what is positive or has the potential to be positive. That habit reinforces a mindset of confidence and allows you to start to notice what is right in the world.

I've always been a huge list maker. I switch between digital tools, paper and pen, my phone and voice memos. Regardless of the tool you use, list making has tremendous power, and if you approach it with adaptability, it can assist you in almost any situation. Making a list of reasons to be confident in yourself, others, the world, and the future can completely reshape your point of view.

The people around you can shape your attitude as well. On one occasion, my son and I were late picking up my daughter from a birthday party. I was rushing him to get his coat on. He'd just finished a Synthesis class in which he was thwarted by complex collaborative computer problems. The teachers had stayed to have a constructive and encouraging troubleshooting session so he could persevere and succeed the next time.

"Let's go, James. We're late,"

He said to me, "Well, it's probably a good thing for her that we're late because she can eat more cake!"

It was so sweet. Instead of taking on my stress about being late, he helped reframe my thinking by highlighting the positive.

The troubleshooting made us late, but it was clearly worthwhile because he went from being despondent and frustrated to giving me a pep talk!

That interaction is one of a myriad of examples of why it's so important to consider your environment and the people you surround yourself with. Their mindset will shape yours, for better or worse. The human mind is like a sponge, picking up everything it touches. We are highly influenceable and impressionable, so we need to use that knowledge of how our minds work to make the best choices.

What If You Can?

Think of all the mountains you could move if you truly believed in yourself and didn't impose any limits. Confidence comes from believing in yourself. If someone else has achieved their dreams or reached the place you want to be, then it's proof that you can, too.

Even if you fall short, you will accomplish significantly more than if you allowed doubt to stop you. Confidence is an accelerating factor, whereas self-doubt and mistrust of others weigh you down like a backpack full of rocks. When you release yourself from the weight, instead of treading water, you become airborne. The modern world requires lightness, flexibility, and agility to adapt in the face of each new change.

Let yourself dream as big as you want to dream. Big for one person might mean becoming the next influential business magnet; for another, it might mean having an awesome team of five people. Paint the vision of what you want, without constraints. You might look at it and think you could never make it real—limiting beliefs rush in almost as quickly as ideas occur. They force us to ask, "What if we can't; what if we fail; what if we make a mistake? What if we embarrass ourselves, someone lets us down or stabs us in the back, or the world changes again before we can reach our target?" I challenge you to ask a better question. *What if I can?*

Genie™ Prompts for Confidence

Go to www.talk2genie.com and type in one of these conversation starters:

- Help me boost my self-confidence
- Let's create a confidence-building plan
- I want to overcome my fear of failure
- Create a daily affirmation routine
- Build my assertiveness skills
- Let's enhance my public speaking confidence
- I want confident body language

Practical Tips to up your game with CONFIDENCE.

Make it real, keep it simple, you're a rock star ☺

These exercises aim to build and boost confidence, both in one-self and in others. They enhance interpersonal relationships by promoting active listening, building empathy, fostering trust, and developing self-assurance. They will help you navigate the challenges of life with increased confidence and resilience.

Constructive Feedback:

Provide constructive feedback and positive encouragement to colleagues, friends, or family members. When someone accomplishes a task or faces a challenge, offer specific, con-structive feedback on their performance. Highlight their strengths and progress, and provide gentle suggestions for improvement. Offering constructive feedback and encour-agement helps others build their self-esteem and confidence. It shows that you believe in their potential for growth. You can also use this same feedback exercise with yourself.

Act as a Mentor or Coach:

Take on the role of a mentor or coach for someone who can benefit from your guidance and support. Identify someone, whether in your professional or personal life, who could ben-efit from your expertise or experience. Providing guidance, advice, and encouragement as they pursue their goals. Acting as a mentor or coach can significantly boost another person's confidence by offering them valuable insights, resources, and a supportive network.

Visualization and Positive Affirmations:

Spend a few minutes each day visualizing yourself confi-dently tackling challenging situations in our accelerating and constantly changing world. Imagine yourself successfully achieving your goals despite uncertainties. Pair this with positive affirmations like "I am capable," "I am adaptable," and "I can handle change." This exercise helps rewire your mindset to be more self-assured and better prepared for unpredictable scenarios.

9

Enthusiasm

The other day as we left school, my daughter gave a big smile to the security guard, known as a gardien in France, as she told him goodbye. He replied, "Goodbye, Little Miss Sunshine." The English nickname fits her well because she's naturally enthusiastic about everything.

Once, in a department store right before New Year's, she zeroed in on a sequined, multicolored dress. I could see the wheels turning in her head: *Wow, that dress really exists. Somebody actually made that. Wait a second. It's in a store, which means technically, my mother could buy it for me.* Sure enough, the dress traveled with us from Paris to Miami, and she wore it for New Year's.

My Little Miss Sunshine engages with the world from a vantage of continual wonder. I often ask myself how I, as an adult, can channel that same wonder, and I work to help my clients do the same. I want them to understand that they can find their version of that sequined dress.

The Power of Enthusiasm

In today's complicated, often exhausting world, enthusiasm is like a secret box of sunshine, an inner light of energy, the fire of joy, a bubbly bottle of champagne you can share with hope and confidence.

Enthusiasm is a highly contagious accelerating force that, like confidence, keeps the wind in your sails as you navigate the world's obstacles, setbacks, and complexities. Without profound enthusiasm about your mission, you lack the bubbly, fiery, happy energy you need to truly dance.

As a leader, whether designated or unofficial, your enthusiasm has great power. It brings the gift of vivacity your team needs to move forward. Your enthusiasm has the capacity to supercharge a situation. When it shines bright, other people will be warmed by it. Like a moth to a flame, enthusiasm attracts, and it inspires others to contribute.

On the flip side, monotone disengagement repels. Your team doesn't need another source of stress. With the impossible to-do lists and shifting sands of today's demands, your team needs enthusiasm now more than ever.

Enthusiasm is Contagious

Samuel Taylor Coleridge said, "Nothing great was ever achieved without enthusiasm." Enthusiasm is like rocket fuel for achievement. It helps overcome stress and frees you to move and dance without worrying about the audience.

Accelerating factors build energy and momentum. Imagine someone filling the basket of your hot air balloon with rocks. Enthusiasm represents the fire that will lift you off the ground. And the best part is its self-perpetuating quality. Enthusiasm gives birth to enthusiasm. With just a little oxygen, the fire of enthusiasm will keep burning.

Enthusiasm comes from within. Positivity is the spark that will light the fire. Then as we harness the recyclable energy, we can help light the fire in others. Because when we ignite enthusiasm in someone else, it's as if two suns align, sending light back and forth. Enthusiasm manifests itself differently in each person, but tapping into your passion can kindle your fire. Harnessing enthusiasm is like finding the secret key to the magic box that's inside you and sharing the contents with yourself and the world.

As a leader and business owner, I continually strive to share sunshine with my clients and my team. They know I will commit the energy necessary to work on their projects in a professional, analytical, pragmatic way. Enthusiasm rescues me from exhaustion and invites me to rise to the occasion.

Enthusiasm also helps me stay in flow with the universe. When I feel annoyed, stressed, frustrated, or tired—as we all do from time to time—the energy of enthusiasm cancels out all the negativity, puts me in the present moment, helps me to connect to other people, and allows me to have real fun.

This fun reveals itself in meetings with clients as we get to the bottom of their learning and development needs, figure out how to boost their sales, or find ways to reinforce their leadership culture. I truly enjoy searching for workable solutions. In those moments, enthusiasm allows us to dance in perfect synchronization as if the problems are choreography showing the avenues to all the different solutions. The world appears open and fluid as I move forward.

You will constantly encounter people who complain, and often, it's somewhat legitimate. Life doesn't always hand us a box of chocolates. However, instead of feeding into that negativity, we can sincerely listen while we lend a light of optimism to the conversation. You will be amazed at the change in countenance of that complainer. Enthusiasm is truly contagious.

The hardships and difficulties people struggle with every single day are real. So, it is a huge and meaningful gift to share positive energy, optimism, and connection with others. Enthusiasm positively impacts the lives of the people around you.

Enthusiasm fosters our resilience to overcome. You can't resolve all of humanity's problems with your ray of sunshine, but your energy and intention do make a difference. Never underestimate the influence a smile or laugh can have on someone who hasn't laughed all day. As you navigate the asteroid field of the day to day, you can radiate energy that will inspire others to proceed toward success instead of pain.

Musicians will tell you they often play better when they are in the company of a higher-level performer. Dancers give more when their partner is all in. The butterfly effect of enthusiasm means that each person you touch will feel inspired to share what they've gained with someone else, and their enthusiasm will inspire the next person. Your enthusiasm has the potential to not only achieve something great for yourself but to also feed someone else's achievement.

Team Enthusiasm

Steve Jobs said, "Great things in business are never done by one person; they're done by a team of people." Building a successful company, completing a change management program, or tackling the biggest issues facing humanity, such as hunger and violence, require a whole community of people working in concert. For that community to have enough determination, intentionality, and speed, we need the light and fire of enthusiasm.

AQai shared a study on positive mindset. Brain sensors found that those with a positive mindset used all regions of their brain while working on a problem, whereas those with a negative mindset did not activate many regions. This neural reality reinforces the need for methods like laugh therapy to change brain chemistry by laughing and smiling.

Creating team enthusiasm means sharing your optimism and excitement. Like any mindset habit, it starts with consciously choosing positivity—even when you don't feel like it. Your choice will encourage your clients and teams to feel excited, too, leading to better results.

I'm not saying smiles and eye contact automatically produce signed contracts, but consciously engaging with enthusiasm certainly improves the energy around a project. Watch what happens when you authentically bring positivity and enthusiasm to the conversation. When you remember to open the box and share what's inside, you'll be amazed at the reaction you can elicit in others.

Cultivating Enthusiasm

John Maxwell said, "Be the most enthusiastic person you know." Even if you tend to be less enthusiastic, you can cultivate that quality. Enthusiasm is the practice of expressing excitement and hope. A natural introvert might need to learn how to demonstrate enthusiasm. It's not that they aren't enthusiastic; however, their personality downplays their excitement. It is possible to train yourself to share your energy through your body language and simple phrases. You don't have to be the caricature of a bouncy cheerleader if that's not your natural personality, but expressing what you think fuels the energy for the project.

On the flip side, if you are naturally extroverted, you may want to make sure that your exuberant energy isn't overpowering your capacity to authentically connect and listen to others. No personality type has a monopoly on enthusiasm.

With conscious effort, you can develop this soft skill. I've spent the past twenty-five years helping people develop things like enthusiasm, and I can tell you that tapping into your reasons for doing the work and practicing them in concrete situations will make them highly accessible and workable for you.

Start each meeting with a positive sentence. A simple compliment can make the difference in your attitude as well as the other person. You can be true to your nature. You'll discover that when you harness your own passion, the energy of enthusiasm lies in your fringes. You won't need a personality transplant. Start by seeing what you would gain if you had more enthusiasm, then work on the skill. Your authenticity will shine. It may feel unnatural, artificial, or superficial at first, but keep trying. Habits, behaviors, and new mindsets are built over time. Every time you look at the positive, you've trained your brain to move toward enthusiasm.

The habit of enthusiasm will not erase who you are or change your DNA. You won't become an extrovert in five days. Nor need you be. But the more you use it, the more comfortable you'll be with it.

The Difference Enthusiasm Makes

Enthusiasm has helped me in countless ways. I use it to rally my coaches when a project turns out to be harder than we anticipated or the client changes their expectations. A one-day project takes five. One client completely rearranges a three-month schedule. Such shifts are extremely common in an environment with a vast array of projects, changing technology, and developing strategies. Without enthusiasm, I can think of many times when people might have let the ball drop or not gone the distance.

My team has a distinct energy that most notice at our first meeting. We have a plethora of highly skilled and competent competitors who do their work with excellence. However, it's our enthusiasm that sets us apart. Clients tell us they can feel our energy, and they want to work with us because they believe in our commitment to their project.

When a program doesn't go well, it's often not because of the structure or content but because it's missing the ingredient of enthusiasm. So, it's vital that the leaders are conscious vehicles of energy.

When we help a company with change-management, we begin by asking people to take risks and be vulnerable so they can build skills that don't come naturally. Their managers may have sent them, and they may not trust the leadership of their company or the benefits of the change-management program.

And while a program will not succeed on enthusiasm alone, the program will also not succeed without that enthusiasm. We work on this concept with many experienced coaches. It's easy to concentrate on the content so vigilantly they lose their sparkle or allow negative energy to steal their shine. You don't need to come out waving pom-poms, but by maintaining enthusiasm, you'll find that people trust you and increase their willingness to participate.

Everyone on my team has genuine, deep, authentic enthusiasm. Some have very bubbly personalities, and others demonstrate it in a more subdued way. But even the most genuine, authentic, experienced, exuberant person can lose their enthusiasm or fail to radiate it. Opening that box is a conscious, voluntary skill you can develop even in the face of stress, resistance, adversity, and distraction.

Obviously, the ballerina doesn't feel like putting every ounce of energy into every performance. Still, the show must go on. Those contrary forces affect us all. Thankfully, our level of enthusiasm is a decision we make rather than something we feel, so we can always choose to lead with enthusiasm.

Genie™ Prompts for Enthusiasm

Go to www.talk2genie.com and type in one of these conversation starters:

- Help me find my passion
- Let's create a daily enthusiasm routine
- I want to stay motivated on long-term projects
- Create a list of inspiring role models
- Build a network of enthusiastic people
- Let's enhance my ability to inspire others
- I want to cultivate a positive mindset

Practical Tips to up your game with ENTHUSIASM.

Make it real, keep it simple, you're a rock star ☺

These exercises are designed to boost enthusiasm, a vital quality for accelerating in a chaotic world. Enthusiasm can fuel motivation, creativity, and resilience, making it easier to tackle challenges and achieve your goals. By integrating these exercises, you can cultivate and sustain enthusiasm, enabling you to approach challenges with energy, creativity, and a resilient spirit.

Passion Project:
Dedicate time to a personal passion project or hobby that excites you. Whether it's painting, writing, or learning a new skill, engaging in something you're passionate about can reignite enthusiasm and inspire creativity, which can spill over into other aspects of your life.

Connect with Inspirational Individuals:
Seek out and connect with people who inspire you. Attend events, seminars, or webinars featuring speakers who have achieved remarkable success or overcome significant challenges. Engaging with their stories and insights can ignite your enthusiasm and provide valuable motivation and guidance.

Self-Observation and Positive Self-Talk:
Develop the habit of self-observation and reinforce your inner dialogue with positive self-talk. Take time to reflect on your thoughts and emotions, making a conscious effort to replace self-doubt and negativity with encouraging and optimistic affirmations. These practices empower you to maintain enthusiasm and resilience, ensuring you thrive in our dynamic and ever-changing world.

10

Mental Flexibility

The flexibility of dancers is amazing. They can do perfect splits and touch one toe to the back of their heads while standing on the other leg. With each leap and lunge, these artistic athletes put their bodies in poses that make many of us cringe. Their arm swings, torso twists, and backbends require an enormous amount of malleability.

When watching the beauty of these performances, few think about the stretching, exercise, and constant practice it takes for these artisans not just to know the routine, but also to be able to move and flow like they do. Being flexible is a skill that dancers develop, and mental flexibility is no different.

When Chocolate Pudding Becomes an Adventure

France had some of the strictest COVID lockdown rules in the Western world. My children and I spent at least ninety days hunkered down in our Parisian apartment without even a balcony for escape. My son had just turned six, and my daughter was not quite two.

The ban on large, in-person gatherings wiped out my business. So, with my daughter on my lap, I set out to reinvent it. I spent my daughter's every napping moment and the hours after she went to bed at my computer because it was the only time I had both hands free.

One project emerged as a financial band-aid for our losses and offered an opportunity for my team to learn how to run programs virtually. We would train more than 1,500 managers in remote management and how to deal with strong emotions in an active virtual workshop format. Given the financial stakes and the huge cultural shift we aimed to orchestrate, the project was beyond stressful.

One day, in order to conduct a phone meeting, I sat my daughter in her highchair with a small jar of delicious French chocolate pudding. She ate a little, but at some point, the cool smooth coagulation must have intrigued her because she started wiping it all over her face. Perhaps it felt like a cool moisturizer.

As I watched, I really wanted to communicate to her that this messy behavior was not acceptable. But the brown goo was keeping her mercifully quiet while I finished the call. I quickly decided the mess didn't matter.

I continued my intense conversation with the client as we tried to fix the issues on the project. Throughout the entire call, I walked around my living room and dining room watching my daughter paint her face and then massage the chocolate sauce into her hair like shampoo.

As it turned out, my daughter painted herself with pudding on more than one occasion—in fact, as often as once a week during that period—because it was one of the only things she could eat on her own. Allowing her that freedom kept her quiet and made a way for me to take the difficult calls required to save my company.

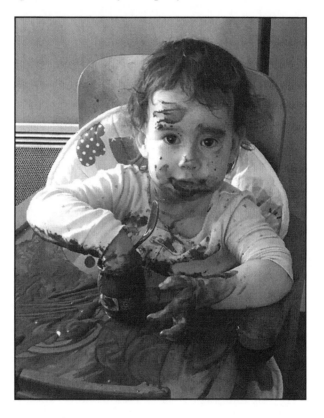

She got into the rhythm of painting, and I got into the rhythm of working while keeping an eye on her. Afterward, I'd give her a bath, and it wasn't a big deal. (On a side note—the entire ordeal has caused my son to swear off dairy products. To this day, he will only eat ice cream. He won't even touch a container of yogurt to put it in the refrigerator.)

My daughter taught me a new aspect of mental flexibility regarding the house rules and my expectations of her as I worked and accelerated the rebuild of my business.

The pandemic lockdowns offered intense opportunities to see everyday actions in a totally different way. Everyone needed to quickly get comfortable juggling new challenges and restrictions as we sorted through contradictory demands and information. Together, with the help of chocolate pudding, my family made it through that surreal period which offered a masterclass in mental flexibility.

What Is Mental Flexibility

Mental flexibility is the capacity to believe more than one thing can be true at the same time. It's also the ability to change your viewpoint quickly, in spite of a long-held belief or hoping for a different path forward.

Mental flexibility means being comfortable with the following statement: "My core convictions are extremely important to me, and I will fight for them," And "I'm open to being challenged about my way of thinking, even when it relates to one of my core convictions."

We face numerous contradictions and a constant stream of seemingly competing demands, perspectives, and information. To enjoy success in the world today, you need to know who you are and what you stand for. Plus, you must accept yourself and hold strong, clear beliefs. At the same time, if you're not open to being challenged or at least willing to give consideration to an opposing viewpoint, you'll get stuck. Mental flexibility gives us the necessary agility to navigate in this world.

Mental flexibility gives us the ability to transition from one task or thought to another quickly and fluidly without draining your energy. Imagine a DJ creating a mix using sliders to crossfade two different tracks—they raise the volume in one track while simultaneously lowering the second. Sometimes we need to do the same—fluidly, just as a DJ does, adjusting our thoughts or switching our actions.

Sometimes in the space of five minutes, you will glance at your phone while you're in a meeting and see an urgent email come in. Meanwhile, you're trying to sort through the different viewpoints of the people in the room (many of which you disagree with) and thinking about how to answer that urgent email. Concurrently, you remember that you need to check with the babysitter, and a team member slips you a note to tell you your Dropbox has been hacked and a client wants a proposal the next morning. Mental flexibility involves using your controls like a DJ, figuring out what to fade in or fade out, and which track comes next.

Cultivating Mental Flexibility

Mental flexibility is inherently connected to adaptability. It helps you work with the pace of change as well as the paradoxes and contradictions of life. On the one hand, we have an exponential curve of technological change. On the other, we're human beings living in biological bodies, navigating through the linear human-built infrastructure and political, school, work, and family systems. The switch makes mental flexibility essential.

Mental flexibility has always had benefits, but they're particularly pronounced today. If you can stay mentally flexible when you receive bad news or negative feedback, you can bounce back quickly. You won't need much flexibility when everything's going well, so when life moves fast and seems to go in a negative direction, we can cultivate mental flexibility by seeing the difficulties as opportunities to practice, stretch, and develop.

In my case, adversity prompted me to reinvent, rebuild, and redo my business processes and our ways of thinking. Because I leaned into mental flexibility, the struggle allowed me to grow.

I got my first hands-on lesson in mental flexibility when I was sixteen and spent a year living in France as an exchange student. The French and the Americans certainly had some similarities, but the culture, language, and history offered pronounced and fundamental differences.

I found myself increasingly frustrated by the lack of understanding between the two cultures. Each side was convinced their way of thinking or doing was the better way, the right way, and the true way—whereas, in most cases, the best course was simply a matter of perspective and preference.

From that young age, I learned two different systems can be equally true. Parisians embark and disembark the Metro in a much different way than New Yorkers get on and off the subway. Children come of age differently in every culture. Again, one way is not necessarily better than another. We're all used to the way of life we grew up with. Those raised in a multicultural setting may naturally have more mental flexibility. To cultivate mental flexibility in yourself, you simply become more aware of and learn to understand the value of different systems—not better or worse, simply different.

The tendency to judge the unfamiliar represents one of the biggest roadblocks to mental flexibility. Americans in France will sometimes judge the smallest customs, such as servers not automatically bringing the check. The French, in turn, may find it rude or rushed for servers to bring the check before they've asked. The two practices are equally valid, but they emphasize different priorities, such as efficiency versus leisure. The French value good meals and social connection while eating, and they believe a restaurant should welcome you and not rush you out. The Americans tend to focus on productivity and pragmatism.

These systems play out in companies, too. The mental filters of a C-Level leader, middle manager, and project manager will reveal their different points of reference. The sooner we understand the reality and importance of each person's referential system, the easier it will be to stay mentally flexible, because, amongst other issues, you won't get caught up in judgment. Seeing things through the lens of another's point of view should pique our interest, and we might find ourselves amused or fascinated by the difference. Mental flexibility allows us to learn from the diversity or even adopt it. In any case, being open to differences will help you accelerate in today's world.

In business this means learning the distinct culture of each company you interact with. If you have awareness of your own referential system and cultivate an understanding of the importance and validity of the new different system, you'll likely get up to speed quickly. You don't have to like all the differences. Your own lens may influence a business that has great mental flexibility. Nevertheless, success requires noticing and adapting to the culture you find yourself in.

For example, at one point, I noticed one of my coaches and a client talking past each other. Again and again, even though the coach was very engaged in the conversation, every time the client asked what the operational value was of a particular program, the coach turned the subject toward emotional intelligence. I pulled the coach aside and pointed out the need to listen to and understand the client; however, the coach believed she understood the client perfectly. It took some prompting for her to understand she was in an EQ frame of mind while the client's referential system was operational management. Once she connected with them within their referential system, she could invite them into ours and offer training that would help them.

When multiple referential systems exist in the same space, it's like the ubiquitous brain teaser of a drawing that, to some people, looks like an old woman and, to others, a young girl. In fact, both images exist simultaneously, and we can teach our brains to toggle back and forth between the two. Reality always comes in multiple layers. Interpretation is subjective. If you can keep your mental filter as open as possible, your mental flexibility will grow, and you'll be able to understand what people are talking about and why they feel what they feel.

Without Mental Flexibility

Lack of mental flexibility will make us tired or cranky. We will feel frustrated by the state of the world and our place in it. The fact is, we often need to think about issues differently than our default. We need to accommodate others' perspectives and integrate their processes in ways that compete with our core beliefs. Life is full of dualities and contradictions. If we're not comfortable being mentally flexible and instead default to rigidity, judgment, and "the way things should be," we'll waste a tremendous amount of energy.

Rigidity also causes us to miss opportunities. We close the door on possibility instead of seizing it and miss out on meeting new people, encountering new ideas, signing new contracts, starting new projects, and making money in different ways. Employers have missed out on the best staff because a tattoo or a piercing shaped their viewpoint before they conducted the interview. Children and adults alike have passed on the most delicious desserts after they heard words like soy, gluten-free, or zero-sugar.

Lack of mental flexibility also leads to communication mishaps. When someone hears or reads a message in one tone without the mental flexibility to consider the person meant something else, communication breaks down and relationships become broken. Understandably, companies prefer to work with mentally flexible people, so those who mount resistance tend to have fewer offers and opportunities.

Adding Improv to the Mix

Theater improvisation relies on an actor's capacity in the moment, under pressure, while other people are watching. I studied theater and communication quite intensively from high school until well into my twenties, which required me to build and strengthen that improvisational muscle on a daily basis.

The cardinal rule of improv is "Yes, and…". Think of how impossible it is to calm a child by telling them to stop crying. On the other hand, if you tap into curiosity, experimentation, and improvisation, the outcome can be completely different.

"What do you think your shoes will feel like on your feet today? Can you put your shoes on faster than me?" Just a couple of questions, and a child will quickly ride a negative wave of emotion into a positive and inquisitive one. That same spirit of improvisation can be productive in our adult, professional lives, too. Every client conversation gives us an opportunity to practice improvisation. We connect best by listening and building on what they're saying.

Working as a trainer and coach has required me to think on my feet and draw on my theater background. When you're training, people are watching and judging you. Companies engage trainers to help their staff develop soft skills that touch on sensitive subjects. My coaches must adapt in a microsecond to the tenor of the group. They have to jump and land on their feet to get it right. Like actors on stage, they read the audience so they can speak to those who resist changing behaviors or mindsets as well as the ones who see the benefit and want to change as quickly as possible. How do you manage those two different rhythms simultaneously?

When recruiting new coaches, I specifically look for professionals who, on top of their knowledge of soft skills and leadership, also have an affirmed confident personality with the capacity to think on their feet, adapt instantaneously, and manage hostile people with total ease. All my coaches have profound mental flexibility. Their capacity to be mentally flexible constitutes a consequential part of what makes our programs so effective and dynamic.

Before I started my company, I co-facilitated a seminar with several other trainers. We were supposed to have a day-long training with set groups of ten managers each, but when we showed up, the client had a different understanding. When I arrived, the head of communications handed me an agenda that required twice as many trainers as we had. She did not hide her belief that we had not shown up prepared. We were way out in the country at a French castle that hosted many trainings and had no way to bring in additional resources.

I quickly took the list of participants and said I'd fix it. I rearranged her list and proposed a way to hit the objectives and deliver meaningful training. If the team I was working with hadn't been flexible, we would have lost that business and created a great deal of disappointment. Mental flexibility helped everyone move forward.

Building Mental Flexibility

We use a number of methods to increase mental flexibility in our training programs. Each one incorporates elements of improv because it helps with a whole system of soft skills. Most people freak out when we tell them they're going to spend an hour and a half on improvisation. They think it's something for trained actors, and they don't want to embarrass themselves. Fortunately, we have talented coaches who know how to help people feel comfortable. In almost every case, participants surprise themselves with their skills. I love watching people surpass their assumed abilities.

Improv involves communicating, taking risks, and being vulnerable. It allows you to noticeably improve your mental flexibility in a short time. As little as an hour can make a huge difference.

Two quick exercises you can do at home or the office are "say yes" and "ask why."

In "say yes," you simply practice saying yes to every problem.

- Yes, they will bring me my check later—and what does that mean?

- Yes, they brought me my check without my asking—and what does that mean?

- Yes, my employee is really focused on their vacation—and why is that important to them?

- Yes, my colleague is really upset—and why is he feeling like this?

Whatever you encounter, try saying yes to open your mind. This allows you to imagine new ways of doing and being.

The "ask why" strategy allows you to flex your reaction when someone approaches a situation in a way that's foreign to you. Sometimes saying yes immediately isn't an option, but no closes the door and causes missed opportunities. "Why" invites openness, flexibility, and new potential solutions.

The "Five Whys" exercise is a simple but powerful tool to identify a problem or objection and then ask why at least five times, chipping away at the layers. If an employee is upset by a client's feedback, for example, ask them why. If you keep asking why people are thinking and acting the way they are, you can get to the heart of the matter and respond accordingly. If you really want to work on this trait, I recommend signing up for an improv class. On top of learning new skills, you'll have so much fun!

When I started my business, I completed a coaching program for young entrepreneurs. The coach had us complete an exercise that has always stuck with me as I find it so valuable. It's a simple exercise involving your hand.

Look at your hand and imagine each finger being one of four solutions to your problem. Then, look at your thumb. Ask yourself, is there a thumb—a fifth, better solution you hadn't thought of yet? If so, go with the thumb. This allows you to open yourself to an even better option, even if you've already worked through other solutions.

In our training programs, we often ask people to force themselves to pitch an opposing viewpoint. Sometimes, they find they're even better at pitching an opposing idea than their own. This exercise is great for cultivating mental flexibility as well as learning how to pitch. Try the exercise with a topic outside your own expertise and content knowledge or even a totally outlandish idea.

For example, we've asked people to take two minutes to explain why everyone in the world should only shower once a month, which has generated some highly compelling pitches. Check out these other pitch worthy ideas that help build mental flexibility.

- Why everyone should wear a bikini to the office in the summer.

- Why we need to free prisoners every weekend.

- Why we should eat only pizza every night for dinner.

The subjects sound ridiculous, but they effectively build mental flexibility, communication, and creativity by pushing us outside our rigid referential system.

Physical actions can also foster mental flexibility because they increase oxygen to the brain. I prefer to walk when I'm engaged in a difficult task. If you need to sit, as on a video call, use hand gestures and facial expressions to help you increase oxygen flow and, by extension, mental flexibility.

I had many stressful calls during those first eight or nine weeks of COVID lockdown, and movement helped me. Often, that meant just walking around my apartment while talking on the phone, taking a five-minute stretch (this feels so good!), or cleaning up toys while conducting business. These activities helped me stay mentally flexible, keep the oxygen flowing, and remain open.

Go Forth, Flexibly

2020 promised to be an amazing financial year. My company had never secured so many large-scale projects. The journey looked exciting, and I felt reassured about my business. Five days in March changed the entire landscape. The bookings evaporated.

One amazing intern who ended up becoming my assistant proved to be extraordinarily fast, mentally flexible, and diligent. She and twenty of my key coaches worked with me to reinvent the business in about six weeks, and we ended the year with twenty-two percent growth.

Netflix(R) gives us an excellent example of mental flexibility and adaptability. When the brand began in 1998, renting DVDs online and having them delivered by mail quickly became a hit. However, as digital products became more popular, the brand moved to streaming and expanded their services worldwide. Since then they have been continuously evolving to meet the demands of the public. While Blockbuster and other video rental giants fell when technology brought chaos into their industry, Netflix thrived because they had the capacity to flex and adapt.

Mental flexibility allows you to use your creativity in ways that serve you and help you solve problems. Online tests can help you determine your level of mental flexibility so you know how to start using what may be your greatest asset for accelerating in the midst of this exponential transformation and dancing through the chaos.

Genie™ Prompts for Mental Flexibility

Go to www.talk2genie.com and type in one of these conversation starters:

- Help me think outside the box
- Let's create a plan to adapt to change
- I want to improve my problem-solving skills
- Create a routine to enhance my cognitive flexibility
- Build a mindset for embracing new perspectives
- Let's enhance my ability to learn from mistakes
- I want to stay adaptable under pressure

Practical Tips to up your game with MENTAL FLEXIBILITY.

Make it real, keep it simple, you're a rock star ☺

Incorporating these exercises into your routine fosters mental flexibility, empowering you to accelerate in the dynamic and unpredictable nature of our world with greater confidence and agility. Developing the ability to handle conflicting ideas and complex situations with ease is essential for success in today's dynamic environment. Developing mental flexibility enables you to think creatively, make agile decisions, and progress toward your goals effectively.

Dialectical Thinking Practice:
Engage in dialectical thinking exercises. These involve examining opposing viewpoints or contradictory ideas and seeking a synthesis or resolution. When confronted with conflicting perspectives, take time to analyze both sides, looking for common ground or new insights. This practice fosters a mindset that can embrace ambiguity and contradictions, enabling you to make more balanced and informed decisions.

Regularly put yourself in others' shoes to understand their viewpoints and experiences. When facing a challenge or making decisions, consider how various stakeholders or team members might perceive the situation. This practice encourages empathy and helps you approach problems with a more open and adaptable mindset.

Iterative Problem-Solving:
Embrace iterative problem-solving by breaking complex challenges into smaller, manageable steps. Continuously assess and adjust your strategies as you gather new information and insights. This approach allows you to adapt and refine your solutions in response to evolving circumstances, improving your mental flexibility in problem-solving.

"Yes, and…" Mindset:
Cultivate a positive and open-minded approach by practicing "Yes, and…" thinking. When presented with ideas or suggestions, respond with "Yes, and…" instead of "No" or "But." Encourage creative thinking and collaboration by building upon others' ideas. Apply this mindset in both personal and professional interactions. "Yes, and" thinking fosters adaptability by promoting a cooperative and innovative mindset, which can lead to better problem-solving and idea generation.

11

Acceptance

Children come into this world with no inhibition and no preconceived prejudices. They accept themselves and others without question. Gradually their adult counterparts train them to keep their clothes on and develop tolerable behavior. By the time these miniature people become teens, they've begun to understand the need to fit in, and they gravitate towards groups they relate to. Being accepted becomes one of the top priorities of teenagers, and too often, it means that these young adults lose their identity to the tribe.

Self-Acceptance

Earlier in my life, I invested way too much time making myself acceptable to those around me. How should I phrase a sentence? Should I copy this person on an email? Distracting questions consumed me: What should I wear? Will I sound silly?

Wasting time agonizing over such inconsequential details is a symptom of not accepting yourself. The same feelings that create wallflowers at a high school prom keep us from fulfilling our dreams and forging ahead in our purpose. This lack of acceptance undermines our confidence and stands in the way of our enthusiasm and mental flexibility. In the absence of self-acceptance, we tend to slide into negative mental chatter, leading us to a small, constrained, unproductive mental space of worrying about every moment when we didn't do or say the perfect thing.

In contrast, when we grow to the point that we accept who we are, we can start to think big about the future. You discover, as Rumi said, "What you seek is seeking you." Accepting who you are means focusing on your positive traits and realizing what you think are negative attributes simply make you uniquely you. When something doesn't go right—you misspeak, for example, or you haven't prepared as much as you wanted to—self-acceptance allows you to own the failures, learn from them, and move forward without dwelling on what went wrong.

At this point in my life, I've learned that accepting who I am allows my uniqueness to shine through—a key strength in an increasingly automated, mass-produced world. Your unique personality and what you bring to the table as an individual represent your greatest value proposition.

Self-acceptance includes recognizing that it's okay to be different. For instance, I talk to my kids about how they're French and American. They live in a single-parent household, and their mother runs a company. Someday those differences may cause them to feel self-conscious or uncomfortable, but understanding the differences before some other child points them out can help them learn to embrace who they are.

I've always had a love for the arts—theater, dance, writing—and when I'm in the company of sports fans that makes me stand out. I used to feel like I should try to change who I was. Even today, I enjoy living in France, and I've embraced the French people, and though I have the nationality, I'm not really French. At the same time, I'm no longer only American. Where does that leave me? I could feel bad or excluded because of my differences, rather, I choose to accept who and where I am. Acceptance starts from what is rather than what we think others expect of us.

Overcoming Imposter Syndrome

Like most people, on more than one occasion when I've started a new endeavor, I've experienced imposter syndrome. I start to second guess myself and wonder if I can measure up. Self-acceptance and confidence are the antidotes; one neutralizes the inner criticism, and the other replaces it with the strength to move forward. Instead of dwelling on what you don't know and what that might say about you, it's okay to show up and acknowledge you don't understand how everything works. By embracing what you don't know as well as what you do, you're empowered to look for support and invest in gaining more knowledge and experience. Self-acceptance facilitates communication and flexibility, it gives you permission to ask questions and grow.

At one point, I brought someone onto the team to fix a particular situation. She started strong, but it turned out she had massive imposter syndrome, and it undermined our ability to collaborate. She'd previously been in a business-to-consumer setting and didn't have experience in a business-to-business model. Plus, our digital component was stronger than she was used to.

Instead of recognizing the differences and asking for help in the areas she found unfamiliar, she clung to her preconceived notions, a defense mechanism for her serious lack of self-acceptance and self-confidence. Had she accepted herself, she would have had the confidence to tell us she didn't know how to manage operational teams or how to use our digital tools. We could have saved considerable time and energy. By not accepting her own limitations and the demands of the environment, she created resistance and a great deal of unnecessary friction.

Accepting yourself makes it easier to accept others. When we begin to understand our own uniqueness and embrace everything we know as well as what we have to learn, we can appreciate those same traits in others. We're no longer in competition with those around us, instead, we see them as people we can learn from and collaborate with to meet all our goals.

To some degree, it's human to struggle with self-esteem, self-acceptance, and doubt. Like so many themes in this book, acceptance is a lifelong journey. Even when you get good at it, you need to keep practicing. Dan Sullivan says of personal growth, "If you're not embarrassed about who you were twelve months ago, then you haven't grown enough." That concept embodies self-acceptance—it recognizes you won't know everything, and outgrowing your shortcomings or your mistakes is part of the process.

Accepting Your Emotions

I was nine years old when I went to overnight camp for the first time. Just before I left, I talked to my mother about being nervous I might get homesick during the seven-week stay. She gave me incredible, lifelong advice that served me during that summer as a young girl and countless times thereafter. My mother gently explained to me that homesickness was a normal feeling. If, from time to time, I felt homesick at camp, I should just go with the feeling, let it flow. Instead of resisting the feeling and trying to push it away, I should accept it and let it be.

I distinctly remember allowing my emotions to simply be that summer. When I felt homesick, I would breathe and imagine the feeling gently flowing through my body and out of my feet. This simple exercise would soothe me and let me connect to my feelings and myself.

Even today when I feel frustrated, sad, or angry, I remind myself to breathe and let the emotion be. Every individual experiences a wide spectrum of emotions, from joy and excitement to sadness and anger. Accepting these emotions as a natural part of life is crucial for self-acceptance. It's important to understand that having a range of emotions doesn't make you weak or flawed; rather, it makes you human. When you acknowledge and accept your emotions, you honor your true self, which is key to building self-esteem and confidence.

Going with the flow of your emotions means allowing yourself to feel them without judgment or resistance. This approach does not mean being controlled by emotions but rather understanding and respecting them as part of your experience. By doing so, you become more in tune with your inner self, leading to greater self-awareness and insight. This self-awareness is a cornerstone of personal growth and resilience.

Embracing your emotions, especially those that make you feel vulnerable, can be challenging but incredibly rewarding. Vulnerability is not a weakness; it's a courageous act of opening up to your true feelings and experiences. By accepting and expressing your emotions, you foster deeper connections with others and cultivate empathy, both for yourself and for those around you.

Consistently accepting and going with the flow of your emotions contributes to long-term mental health. It helps reduce stress, anxiety, and the risk of emotional burnout. When you are at peace with your emotions, you're more likely to have a positive outlook on life, be more creative, and find it easier to navigate life's challenges. Accepting your emotions and allowing yourself to experience them fully is a bold act of self-acceptance; it's a profound step towards a healthier, more fulfilling life. It's about embracing the full range of the human experience and using it as a foundation for growth and connection.

Accepting Your Environment

The world can often feel like a disorienting whirlwind of change and competition. It's tempting to complain that you don't have enough time, can't rely on others, and always have to pick up the slack. But complaining about change will not influence your environment. If you want to play a role in the current and future configuration of the world, embracing abundance rather than succumbing to scarcity, you must accept the reality of your environment.

You cannot find abundant opportunity from a place of negativity. Yes, you'll need to get things off your chest from time-to-time, but those impulses can't set the overall tone. Without acceptance, you'll be the little mouse on a wheel instead of the dancer in control of the stage.

Resistance and lack of acceptance also bring down those around you—your team, your collaborators, your network. To move forward, we must start where we are instead of wishing we were somewhere else.

Accepting our environment includes recognizing its constant change. Acceptance allows us to adapt at an exponentially increasing pace. Our world becomes more interconnected every day. So, every change impacts more than we can comprehend. Coming to terms with the way the world is and the fact there is no end in sight to this accelerating change lets us navigate and accelerate. Until you accept, you can't even get started.

Choose Your Environment Wisely

While accepting our environment is imperative to acceleration, moving out of unhealthy locations and relationships is even more vital. There are a few things to consider when evaluating your environment. First, if you find it unhealthy now, did it work for you previously? Often, change causes discomfort—maybe you can help accelerate the change. Second, a new environment might trigger imposter syndrome. If so, you probably need time to adjust. Lean into your confidence and acceptance to get up to speed. However, if the environment is toxic because it's full of people who don't accept the reality of the world, don't value your contribution, or don't mesh with your core values, then you should find a new environment.

I certainly don't advocate leaving at the first sign of difficulty, because even the most amazing organizations and relationships go through rough patches and hard times. However, in the case of a fundamental mismatch that will thwart your ability to progress and thrive, it's time to make a change. Seek out an environment and community with a perspective on the world that will allow you and the organization to remain in flow. Those organizations, leaders, and teams exist.

One key is searching for people who focus on the positive and are future focused. For example, neurologist Rudolph Tanzi has been focused on Alzheimer's research since his days at Harvard Medical School. In the past thirty years, he's helped identify seventy-five genes that are connected to the development of the disease. He has accepted the current environment in order to improve upon it. Tanzi and others like him show us that accepting the environment does not mean being resigned to it, but acknowledging where we are gives us the power to move forward.

One of the speakers at Abundance360 started a rocket company now valued at over $2 billion. He described the scariest moment in running his company: two weeks before locking in a new round of funding, his team accidentally blew up the rocket while it was on the ground. Mistakes are an inherent part of the entrepreneurial journey. Moving beyond them requires acceptance of your environment, allowing you to leverage your unique strengths and find the people who can help you recover and carry on.

Accept your environment and surround yourself with people who accept it. That acceptance promotes a positive mindset, encourages enthusiasm, harnesses perseverance, and unleashes all manner of other skills you can't otherwise access. By contrast, from the place of resistance and close-mindedness, the biggest, most future-oriented initiatives of our time—from going to Mars to curing dementia—seem impossible, pointless, too hard, or too complicated. Without acceptance, it's easy to get stuck and miss out on the beauty of the dance.

Genie™ Prompts for Acceptance

Go to www.talk2genie.com and type in one of these conversation starters:

- Help me accept things I cannot change
- Let's create a plan to embrace uncertainty
- I want to improve my self-acceptance
- Create a routine for practicing gratitude
- Build a mindset for accepting feedback
- I want to accept others as they are
- Develop strategies for accepting change

Practical Tips to up your game with ACCEPTANCE.

Make it real, keep it simple, you're a rock star ☺

These exercises are crafted to nurture your capacity for self-acceptance, acceptance of others, and a broader acceptance of our world. Embracing these qualities is vital for navigating the unpredictable and complex nature of our world. As you develop acceptance, you'll become more resilient and adaptable, fostering harmonious relationships and constructive interactions in the face of uncertainty and diversity.

Self-Compassion and Embracing Imperfection:
Practice self-compassion by treating yourself with kindness and understanding, especially during challenging times. When facing setbacks or uncertainties, be mindful of your inner dialogue and avoid self-criticism. Instead, speak to yourself as you would to a friend, acknowledging your imperfections and accepting that setbacks are a natural part of life. This exercise nurtures self-acceptance and strengthens your capacity to navigate adversity.

Challenge the pursuit of perfectionism by deliberately engaging in activities where you intentionally make mistakes or create imperfect outcomes. This exercise helps you become more comfortable with the idea that not everything needs to be flawless. Embracing imperfection fosters a sense of acceptance and flexibility when faced with unexpected results or setbacks.

Letting Go Ritual:
Dedicate a few minutes each day to a letting go ritual. Reflect on any worries, regrets, or anxieties you may be holding onto and consciously release them. This practice can be as simple as taking a deep breath and visualizing these concerns dissipating. It promotes acceptance by encouraging you to release the grip on things beyond your control and focus on the present.

Feelings and Needs:
Practice identifying and expressing your feelings and needs, and actively listen to others in conversations to identify theirs. During a conversation, pause to become aware of your own feelings. Are you feeling frustrated, anxious, or content? Identify the specific emotion you're experiencing.

Next, identify the underlying need or desire related to that feeling. For example, if you're feeling frustrated, your need might be for understanding or cooperation. Express your feelings and needs using "I" statements. For instance, "I feel frustrated because I need more clarity in our communication." When the other person speaks, listen actively to identify their feelings and needs. Avoid judgment or making assumptions about their emotions or desires.

Reformulate what you've heard by saying something like, "I hear that you're feeling [emotion] because you have a need for [need]. Is that correct?"

Continue the conversation by exploring possible solutions or compromises that meet both parties' needs. This exercise, based on Non Violent Communication techniques, helps you and others communicate with greater empathy and understanding. By focusing on feelings and needs, it fosters acceptance and constructive problem-solving, reducing conflicts and enhancing relationships, which is particularly valuable in a complex and shifting world.

12

Competition

Competition has been a chief accelerating component since the beginning of time. Ancient historians tell tales of wars of conquest as tribes competed for the best land and biggest area in which to live. In the mid-1900s, competition between the United States and the Soviet Union pushed up the timeline of space exploration as both nations raced to be the superior country in that arena.

In the area of the arts, orchestra musicians practice diligently to move into higher chairs. Dancers accelerate their skills to be ready for competitions, and in ballet companies, the opportunity to become the principal dancer or the prima ballerina drives a competitive spirit between the members.

Fortunately, competition doesn't have to be cut-throat or zero-end-game with a single winner. Healthy competition can co-exist with, and even fuel, collaboration, co-elevation, and abundance.

The Positive Power of Competition

Humans need healthy competition. Unfortunately, many mistakenly believe that it somehow operates in opposition to collaboration and cooperation. But healthy competition challenges us to level up. Society has begun to shy away from competition because people worry—often for good reason—that it fosters exclusivity, disrespect, and deceit. But if we raise awareness of those pitfalls, we can actually enjoy competition.

The camp I attended in my youth, which my son now attends, hosts a "Color War" each Summer. The four-day event can be pretty intense, but it demonstrates the way competition can be extremely constructive. During my camp years, Color War became the highlight of every summer. Though we knew the game would begin near the end of our time together, it always broke out in a surprise fashion. Anticipation of the two teams duking it out brought as much joy as the game itself.

One of the beautiful things about this ferocious war was the way the battle brought an element that most find lacking in a competitive atmosphere—inclusion. Inclusion is a worthy goal, but it's important to understand that inclusion and competition are not diametrically opposed. Constructive competition brings out the best ideas and helps humanity move forward. In Color War, even girls like me who neither enjoyed nor excelled in sports shined because the competition and comradery pushed everyone to perform at their highest level—whatever that was. The games included scavenger hunts, intense athletic events, swim and track meets, relay races, and more. There were no participation trophies, but each person was only expected to do their best.

From day one, the camp emphasized that sportsmanship and how we treated others was of utmost importance, so our war taught us to be good winners as well as good losers. Everyone brought their most intense effort and positive spirit. Competition and positivity existed simultaneously, creating strong engagement, commitment, and motivation. Working together to win caused an inclusive bond to develop in the process. Years later, I still have a special connection with adults who shared that childhood experience with me—even those from the other team.

My company runs pitch workshops for our clients. Each one ends with teams participating in a competition. Clients often ask to skip that portion of the workshop. Some leaders fear competition could undermine collaboration among managers and lead to a sense of exclusion or rank. However, the childish game-like design—often performed on a corporate stage, with the human "applaud-o-meter" determining the vote in a silly manner at the end—helps people chill out and reduces the risk of cutthroat behavior. At the same time, the opportunity to pitch in front of a crowd produces enough adrenaline that participants commit on a higher level and perform better. Since humans tend to be innately competitive, our game allows managers to practice managing the stress that inevitably accompanies collaboration with competitive personalities.

When clients insist that they don't want any form of competition, I explain our rationale, and we abide by the client's wishes. Still, I believe they miss out on harnessing the positive power of competing.

Innovation and Relationships in Competition

Competition driven by the play-to-win mindset we talked about earlier promotes innovation and strong relationships. Every hurdle becomes an invitation to be creative because we believe something bigger or better awaits. That's why some top performers compete against themselves. Runners know that simply trying to beat their own best time offers enough positive competition to push them to be better.

The culmination of Color War was the song and cheer competition on the last evening. For four days, campers brought forth every bit of innovation and creativity to bring four songs to life—a fight song, a cheer song, a comedic song, and the Alma Mater. A jury of directors and senior counselors would decide the ultimate winner, and because the stakes were so high in this final phase, both teams had an equal chance of taking home the prize. Every camper memorized, rehearsed, and became accustomed to the unique rhythm of each tune.

At the conclusion, the judges would announce a winner, and the entire group moved to the center of the rec hall with the Camp Evergreen cry. Winners and losers alike shed tears as the tension of the competition subsided. We hugged and sobbed as we realized that camp would be ending, knowing we wouldn't see these good friends we'd made for at least another ten months.

Each summer at camp, we all gathered around a campfire to start and conclude the season. At the end of the opening campfire the first evening of camp, the director had us look left and then right. She explained that these people would likely be our friends forever. Between my years of being a camper and a counselor, I experienced about twelve of those first evening gatherings. The director was correct, some of those girls are still my friends—regardless of what team we ended up on and who won or lost.

When a healthy-competition mindset is imparted in the workplace, the energy it creates can be invaluable. I don't remember Color War ever causing fights or dissension. A huge factor in that fact is the value placed on making and maintaining lifetime friends. The camp constantly instilled the importance of the relationships we formed. From a young age, I understood that the friendships were more important than winning, especially at key moments such as when the pressure of Color War and the drive to achieve and win ruled the day.

Working together as a team to succeed builds relationships and creates strong bonds. My team wins many bids, and it's important to celebrate those wins. But sometimes we lose, and I believe it's equally important to celebrate in the midst of the losses. Even after a loss, we can celebrate that we put forth our best effort. If we missed something, we can debrief and celebrate that we've learned something incredibly helpful, useful, or profitable for the next attempt. I've learned some of my most valuable lessons through losing competitive bids. Sure, it stings to lose, but that was one of the tremendous lessons from camp—losing is hard, but it's not the end—it's okay to absorb that loss as well as its lessons and move on.

Business owners and leaders can create a relationship driven culture in their companies. Our trainings help foster this mindset, but corporate executives who model this people-first mentality can also provide opportunities for competition that will accelerate their company's impact and income. When people feel valued regardless of outcomes, competition, and collaboration can comfortably reside in the same box.

Healthy competition also requires some vulnerability. As I mentioned, I wasn't very athletic. So, Color War pushed me to look a little foolish and put myself into situations where I knew even if I did my best, I wouldn't be the best. However, the relationships I built prior to our battle gave me the courage to take the risk because I knew I would have support from my friends even when I looked silly.

Going all in regardless of the outcome can be daunting. There's a risk to taking action in such a public sphere because people will know if you fumble. And that is a risk that comes along with a constructive, collaborative, co-elevating environment. The good news is that when we take risks and allow ourselves to be vulnerable, we end up feeling better if we lose because we don't have to wonder if we could have produced a different outcome if we'd taken a bigger chance. Vulnerability helps us avoid regrets, but more than that, it strengthens bonds because those you're vulnerable with sense that you trust them.

Healthy Competition

In your business, healthy competition begins with understanding that everyone is looking for the same outcome. Healthy competition challenges everyone to bring their best, at the same time, each person understands that their idea may not win. Instead, it might fuel someone else's concepts.

Jeff Bezos told Harvard Business Review that knowing competition was hot on his heels spurred Amazon to be creative. With every new innovation, Amazon's competition created a similar product within two years. Knowing he had that two year timeline pushed the company to forge ahead and be strategic in their marketing. [20]

Peter Diamandis's nonprofit, the X PRIZE Foundation, organizes innovation competitions to encourage technological development that will benefit humanity. Independent small groups or organizations consistently beat industry records previously held by the giants. Amateurs working out of their garages figure out how to clean up oil spills faster than Shell or Chevron. In other instances, competitors have sent rockets into space and addressed some of humanity's biggest concerns, such as ensuring access to clean water. The X PRIZE competition focuses on the solution rather than who comes up with it first. The small teams innovate and build more effectively, and the competition offers a great way to break through big barriers in very short periods of time.

Engaging competition and co-elevation also requires an acceptance of failure. If you learn to see the wins within the losses, the concept of failure disappears. You see every competition as an opportunity for growth and improvement regardless of the outcome.

This approach has impacted my own business and strategy. We see every competition as a chance to leverage past lessons, learn new ones, and level up. I lead with positive energy to engage and motivate my team. And because our focus is learning collaboratively rather than winning by any means necessary, our team can identify problems and help them progress. Most people fail to bring their best because they grapple with fear and a need to control the outcome. Using every new process as a chance to improve allows my team to work on those issues.

My Competitive Nature

I've always had a competitive nature, which reveals itself in a variety of ways, but nearly always involves me going all in. Going all in ups the game. It often means you're fighting off imposter syndrome about your skill set, ability, mindset, intelligence, and likeability. It involves vulnerability, courage, tapping into self-confidence, and self-acceptance to harness what you need to bring your best self.

Over the course of my life, I have had moments of less self-confidence when I didn't play to win. However, when I've stuck my neck out and taken the risk despite my nervousness, I've had more wins. Mindset matters. Even when I lose, I feel better if I've left it all on the field. Winning always feels good. Nevertheless, loss is inevitable, but even losing can be fulfilling, knowing you gave yourself fully to the endeavor.

I think that's why I found Color War so rewarding. Everyone gave their all, and when it was over, we huddled for hugs and sobs regardless of which team we were on. Because everyone had given their best, no one had any regrets, and the last night of camp, with the competition of Color War fresh in our memory, we celebrated.

That closing campfire commemorated the highlights of our summer, and campers from both teams shared the presence of their friends one last time before getting back on the buses to go back home.

Decades later, the enormous camp family still surrounds me despite having moved an ocean away. The memories are extremely vivid and so ingrained in who I am that I often look to those experiences for inspiration on how I can create the same strength of community in my professional situations.

When I train my coaches on new projects, I always conduct a pilot run. They face client evaluations, comparisons against other providers, and the potential to find flaws that need to be addressed before we roll it out. As they aim for excellence and concentrate on making sure the project has no bugs, it's common for them to get nervous and call me three days before the deadline to say they're feeling too much pressure. The simple act of getting the worry off their chest helps them perform.

My company works with this type of competition and fear to help our staff and clients grow to their full potential, so they can achieve top results. The added dose of competitiveness helps us perform at a higher level. We're always trying to meet the mark and then set a new standard.

People who care and stay engaged will naturally be nervous. My team takes the edge off and keeps the competition positive by staying connected to the altruistic goal of helping people with essential soft skills. When you include competition in your method, you enter a process of continual improvement.

Competition Raises the Bar

Without competition, we run the risk of underperforming. In an effort to avoid hurt feelings, we've lowered the standards in some sectors. While no one expects less than the best from professional dancers, performers, and athletes, in other areas, we tend to let it slide if someone is doing less than their best. We have become so concerned about hurt feelings or perceptions of exclusion that people are giving less than their best. Lower expectations create an inability to thrive, particularly in schools.

Machines replaced men and women in factories decades ago. AI and robotics continue to perform tasks formerly reserved for humans. Why do we demean the mass potential of humans to surpass our technological counterparts? As it becomes easier and easier to replace human actions and contributions, we need to level up to protect what is unique about our species and engage with the ethical and strategic questions behind new technologies. We have a responsibility to raise the bar.

Bring Out the Genius

Competition allows us to acquire higher standards. I'm not talking about working longer and harder but rather making the mental shift to elevate and bring out the genius in people.

If life is Dancing with the Stars, then our success means learning life's choreography, being pushed out of our comfort zones, and performing at the top level every week. The only way to break through the difficulty and the barriers we face is to harness our inner Anna Pavlova and dance like we have nothing to lose.

Technology and AI have pushed our culture into hyperdrive, but the truth is these machines only know what humans program. They search the information they've been fed at unimaginable speeds and can even learn to mimic our speech and anticipate what we might say or do. However, they are limited to the ingenuity programmed by humans.

Human brains need to engage as much as possible. The speed of technology gives genius an advantage because the ideas we conceive can be processed faster and put through artificial testing to tell us what needs to be improved. Nothing has the power to speed the process and reveal the kind of genius necessary to innovate for a better world than competition.

I don't want to in any way diminish kindness, positive reinforcement, inclusion, diversity, collaboration, or cooperation, but it's possible to have trophies and winners without excluding anyone. Decades later, I still think fondly of those camp competitions. I learned how to win with grace and lose in a constructive, safe environment. I talked so much about the experience that by the time my son was old enough to participate, he was unbelievably excited.

Watching James enjoy his summer at Evergreen's brother camp, Kenwood, brings me great joy. My daughter Marianna will be starting in a couple years. I am profoundly happy to know my children will experience the same depth of friendship, positivity, diversity, and core values I learned as a youth.

With the right mindset, competing promises benefits that far outweigh any negatives. Healthy competition lets us shine as we bring out our best selves. Plus, when we compete with positivity and the big picture in our sights, we also inspire the best self of those around us.

Genie™ Prompts for Competition

Go to www.talk2genie.com and type in one of these conversation starters:

- Help me with developing a competitive mindset
- Let's create a plan to improve my performance
- I want to learn from my competitors
- Create a routine for staying motivated
- Build a strategy for healthy competition
- I need to be more resilient in competitive environments
- I want to balance competition and collaboration

Practical Tips to up your game with COMPETITION.

Make it real, keep it simple, you're a rock star ☺

These exercises are tailored to enhance your competitive spirit and strategic thinking in a complex and fast-moving world. They inspire innovation and drive progress, helping you excel and thrive within the dynamic and competitive landscape of our intense environment. By incorporating these practices into your routine, you'll cultivate a "play to win" mindset, boosting your confidence, determination, and ability to achieve your goals with unwavering focus and adaptability.

Mindset Reframing:
Challenge and reframe your mindset regarding competition. Instead of viewing competitors as threats, see them as opportunities for growth and improvement. Embrace competition as a motivator that pushes you to excel and innovate. When faced with competitive challenges, remind yourself of the valuable lessons and personal growth that can result from

such experiences. This exercise helps shift your perspective and encourages a positive and competitive spirit.

Competitive Visualization and Mental Rehearsal:
Before important competitions or challenges, immerse yourself in focused visualization and mental preparation. Picture yourself in the midst of the event, flawlessly executing your strategies and emerging triumphantly. Visualize the sensation of success and the rewards it brings, whether it's acing a job interview, delivering a compelling presentation, or conquering a sports competition. This exercise helps program your mind to automatically adopt a "play to win" mindset empowering you to perform at your best under pressure.

Competitive Accountability Buddy:
Partner with a trusted friend, coach, or mentor who can hold you accountable for maintaining a "play to win" mindset. Share your goals and competitive aspirations with them. Regularly discuss your progress and challenges, seeking their guidance and encouragement. Having an accountability partner helps you stay committed to your competitive mindset and ensures you have someone to provide support and feedback.

PART THREE

Navigational Skills

13

Perseverance

What would we do without the navigational systems of the twenty-first century? New drivers can't imagine printing out directions from the computer, nevermind using a full-blown map. On the other hand, most of us have grown quite reliant on the GPS built into our cars and phones.

These navigational devices have become the choreography of our lives. Like the step-by-step instructions of a dance routine, we need something to guide us, to help us arrive at our final destination. Rooted in hope, courage, focus, relationships, creativity, and practice, we have adaptability, confidence, enthusiasm, mental flexibility, acceptance, and healthy competition to help move us forward. Now we need something to keep us going in the right direction.

Navigating with Perseverance

When GPS devices first came out, people joked about how they never gave up. If you made a wrong turn, the artificial voice would let you know— "recalculating route." Sometimes the next instructions would take you around a block, and other times you would need to turn around; however, regardless of how many erroneous turns you made, the little box would keep giving you directions until you got back on track.

That's perseverance at work. In this fast-paced world, it's so easy to take a wrong turn. After a few attempts at getting on the right road, we're tempted to give up. Perseverance continually reroutes us. It reminds us to keep trying.

How many projects are you involved in every day? Two? Two hundred? And with each one, it seems like someone keeps rewriting the choreography every ten steps. Just when we think we have the dance sequence figured out, the goal changes, the deadline moves, or the client decides to start from scratch. Perseverance is the first of our navigational tools that will keep us from being pulled in a million directions.

As the learning landscape has changed in business, my company has had to reinvent itself on numerous occasions. I could easily give up and refuse to adapt. But with every exponential advancement, my team pushes ahead. We collaborate through the growing pains, try new approaches, and test innovative solutions. By looking ahead at what's possible, we can press on to our new destination.

For instance, a client was trying to close a $100 million deal that involved high-stake politics and the implementation of complex technological solutions. He invited the ten stakeholders who would be making the decision to join his team at a hotel to hammer out the issues, roadblocks, and doubts concerning his proposal. They spent the weekend on this process, without any guarantee of finding a solution and moving forward—it was a big ask, with a clear risk of failure. But they did it. My client demonstrated commitment and what I'd call "flagrant perseverance." That level of perseverance impressed the client, and his company won the project.

Perseverance attracts people. When a client, boss, or child sees that you won't give up or abandon them when the going gets tough, they have more confidence in you. They know when you face a few extra miles—or a few thousand extra miles—you'll see it through. In today's turbulent times, this skill is crucial to success.

The Fuel for Perseverance

Like an ultramarathon runner or a rider in the Tour de France, you need an internal source of ongoing energy. These athletes can't just coast. They must create their own momentum. When their muscles burn, and they feel like they have nothing left, perseverance pushes them to the finish line. Perseverance keeps you progressing at full speed in the right direction and sharpens your reflexes.

But where does the fuel for perseverance come from? Let's circle back to the Introduction of this book. We talked about defining your purpose. What gets you out of bed every morning? A ballerina without a drive to be the best will never learn pointe. Until they learn the correct posture, it's quite painful. Playing a stringed instrument provides similar challenges. Without a deep desire to learn the guitar, mandolin, or violin, they'll give up too soon. Calluses will give the musician the ability to fly over the strings but getting them requires that internal fuel.

Star athletes have it, prima ballerinas have it, professional bluegrass players, and TED talk speakers have it. Deep within, something drives them. They have purpose. It may morph or evolve over the years; however, that deep desire fuels their perseverance.

Howard Schultz had every reason to give up. He applied for loans at more than two hundred banks over the period of a year before finding a couple of doctors to help him with start-up money. Without perseverance, Starbucks wouldn't exist. A newspaper publisher told Walt Disney he lacked creativity on the day he fired the entertainment giant, and Mickey Mouse was rejected by Hollywood. Fortunately, Mr. Disney wouldn't give up. [21]

If you have children, you know that even parents have that internal source of energy that navigates their actions. My son didn't sleep through the night until he was two-and-a-half. During one phase, I tucked him in at 8:30 p.m. and then repeated the process twenty-five or thirty times. Sometimes, there would be thirty minutes or an hour between attempts; other times, I'd leave his room, and twenty seconds later, he'd reappear. On more than one occasion, we were still up at 5:00 a.m.

I tried the nice, calm method; the screaming, not-so-nice method; and everything I could think of in between. I was absolutely exhausted, and so was he. His daycare center, known as a "crèche" in France, had a policy not to wake kids from a nap. He'd arrive at the crèche so exhausted that he'd often sleep for three hours at a stretch. Then he'd return home from the crèche and wouldn't be tired at bedtime. It was a vicious, sleep-deprived cycle.

For my sake as well as his, I refused to give up. We focused on getting him to sleep through the night, and eventually, we succeeded. But it took energy that stemmed from love for my son and my desperate need for sleep to help us persevere during that trying time.

If you feel like you lack momentum, it may be time to go back and reevaluate your goals. They might need to be adapted to the ever-changing world. Or perhaps they need a complete rewrite. Your lack of perseverance might be a sign you're not going in the right direction.

In order to persevere, we need a certain amount of sheer force, like a rocket defying both wind and gravity to exit the atmosphere. When you have a defining purpose, you will have sufficient power, nothing can knock you off course.

Some projects and objectives may feel outside your over-arching purpose. To fuel them, look for teachable moments in the project or watch for ways they can tie into your purpose. Sometimes, things slightly off target can be stepping stones toward your larger goal. By using mental flexibility to see them in a different light, you can generate energy to keep going.

The constant change and reinvention of your plans may make you feel like you're drowning and can't reach the surface. Failure will steal your energy, especially during those times when it feels like no matter what you do, it's not right. During those times, remember your why. Then you can put your head, heart, soul, mind, and body into it—and go. Envision the light at the end of the tunnel and the positive outcome, even if you don't know exactly how you're going to get there. That forward propulsion will motivate you and help mobilize those with you. In the face of failure, frustration, and fatigue, your reason for existing will propel you.

Grit, Commitment, and Engagement

Early in my business, my attention was always divided. Some moments were easier than others, but I had to persevere. At one point, an anticipated outcome didn't materialize, and I complained to my father on the phone. He said, "Put your head down, get through it, and do it."

My father was pointing to grit, which—along with drive and determination—is a distinct but linked skill to perseverance. The word grit sounds like dirt and abrasion. When you add grit to perseverance, you can get through the dirty and abrasive obstacles.

Grit comes into play when you can't just coast but need to dig deep to find your source of energy. On those days when we need a grit style of perseverance, we find two additional factors—the pleasure of winning and trying to avoid pain.

Mountain climbers and ultramarathoners use grit. So do double amputees running in the Special Olympics. In addition to their purpose, the joy they find when they cross the finish line helps drive them. It's difficult for most people even to imagine the sheer determination and grit it takes to compete in those events. Even the practice it takes to get started requires perseverance. People with a strong command of these skills don't let a disability stop them.

Commitment and engagement work with perseverance. Without commitment, why would you bother making the effort? There are times you lose sight of the prize or it doesn't look as shiny. When that happens, it's tempting to feel like your goal doesn't matter. Maintaining the status quo looks easier. We all have those moments of doubt, but commitment keeps us in the game and reconnects us to our perseverance and grit.

My Personal Experience with Perseverance

I'm no stranger to setbacks. I can't count the number of times I've encountered unanticipated difficulties and obstacles over the years. Setbacks can deplete you emotionally, especially when you put blood, sweat, and tears into the project, but your attempts don't seem to work—or they work for a while and then fall apart.

For instance, I've signed major contracts, only to have the budget canceled. We've launched effective programs and then had a key coach withdraw for personal reasons. I've hired people who haven't performed as expected in key jobs, invested in new tools that don't work, and implemented strategies that cost us time, money, and energy, only for them to fail. Without the force of perseverance, the business would have crumbled. Our success relies on the drive to continue forward.

Persevering doesn't have to involve business or lofty goals; it can also be as simple as teaching a toddler. Children make for wonderful reminders of the value of perseverance because they're biologically built to test limits. We must persevere through the complaining, the begging, the manipulation, and the tantrums.

It would often be much easier in the moment to capitulate and give a child whatever they want. Caving could allow you to cook dinner, return a call to a client, or just have a peaceful break for ten minutes. However, perseverance taps into your larger purpose and longer-term goal of raising a well-adjusted child into an adult. When you're exhausted, it takes perseverance to deny your child the bowl of ice cream they want an hour before dinner.

I'm always busy, but when I hit the wall of feeling overwhelmed, I put my head down and know I'll get through it. At the same time, I zoom out to identify structural issues that may be causing the problem.

When the company grows, but we have not yet adapted the structure, or we've underestimated the workload of a project, it can feel like I'm sinking. Instead, I have to look for ways to strategically fix the situation. Perseverance doesn't mean you have to work your way through the problems without finding solutions. There are almost always several ways of reaching an objective; it's just a matter of persevering to find the right one.

After our business made it through the first year, my assistant and I began to generate more sales and land more clients. The pace picked up relatively quickly for such a small enterprise. Soon, I had to hire three external coaches to run programs, allowing me to step back from direct facilitation.

We made progress, but it was hard work without a salesperson, a coaching team, or the other resources we have today. By our third year in, I projected revenues would double; however, a big recession hit that year, and clients saw our services as non-essential. All anyone could talk about was the financial crisis and banks crumbling.

I persevered by pivoting from communication and sales to responding to the needs of our clients. A company approached me and wanted to internationalize its management curriculum, a service its current provider could not deliver. I said yes, we could absolutely do such a training.

My enthusiasm aside, the project took a significant amount of manpower without a huge financial upside to match. I had never designed management content, and our coaches had never delivered management training. We had to design and create an entire international management curriculum, as well as find and onboard coaches with different profiles, all in a very short period of time.

My team persevered through the many late nights. They tapped into the momentum, energy, drive, and motivation. I consider that reinvention a major milestone because it shaped the direction of the company. The decision also opened a tremendous number of doors. The way we design and run management and leadership curriculums today is entirely different than when we began, but they have become our largest source of income.

We persevered, adapted, and ultimately prevailed. It was unimaginably difficult, but we weathered the storm and redefined the business for the better.

Your Adventure with Perseverance

Pursuing perseverance means you have some sort of goal. Perseverance supports achievement, and without it, you will not successfully navigate the collision of the exponential technological and linear human curves.

To improve the skill, you will need a clear sense of purpose. Go back to the introduction and ask those questions that help you define your why. You also must be able to accept that things don't always work the first, second, third, or fourth time. Still, you keep trying. This skill requires the mental flexibility to look for and expect adversity so you can tackle it head-on, as well as develop a positive attitude toward obstacles.

To-do lists help us persevere. Seeing everything written down so we know exactly what we need to do calms the mind. Operationally, we all have more to do than we can organize from memory alone. Trying to keep it all in the brain can overwhelm us.

Creative management also makes for a great perseverance builder. When you encounter an obstacle or your energy flags, consider ways to manage it, get around it, or reroute entirely. When we tap into our why, we can harness our grit and determination, and creatively manage ways to the other side.

Dan Sullivan talks about the dangers of hitting The Ceiling of Complexity. After, or even before, you reach your goal, it's important to set a new one so you can keep moving forward. Breaking through that ceiling requires perseverance, and something new on the horizon is often a great catalyst to help you make it to the finish line.

Finally, give yourself some recognition. Acknowledge that the work you do is hard, but it's also important, so it's worth all the striving. Celebrate your efforts even when others don't notice. That can be a lonely place. Acknowledging and celebrating your perseverance will motivate you to continue.

Genie™ Prompts for Perseverance

Go to www.talk2genie.com and type in one of these conversation starters:

- Help me with staying committed to my goals
- Let's create a plan to overcome setbacks
- I want to build my resilience
- Create a routine for daily perseverance practice
- Build a mindset for long-term perseverance
- Help me stay motivated during tough times
- I want to maintain perseverance in team settings

Practical Tips to up your game with PERSEVERANCE.

Make it real, keep it simple, you're a rock star ☺

These invigorating exercises are tailor-made to turbocharge your perseverance, empowering you with the unshakable resilience and unwavering determination needed to conquer the thrilling twists and turns of a fast-changing and complex world. They not only build your capacity to persist through challenges but also enhance your adaptability, making you better prepared to tackle the ever-changing landscape with confidence and composure.

Resilience Strengthening:
Develop your ability to bounce back from setbacks by practicing resilience-building exercises. Reflect on past challenges
you've overcome and the lessons you've learned. Cultivate a
growth mindset by embracing failures as opportunities for
growth. Engage in stress-reduction techniques like mindfulness meditation or deep breathing exercises to help you stay
calm under pressure.

Birds of a Feather Flock Together:
Surround yourself with a strong support network of friends,
family, mentors, and colleagues who share the trait of perseverance. Share your goals and challenges with them, and
seek their advice and encouragement when facing difficulties. Connecting with others who share your aspirations and
determination can boost your motivation and provide valuable insights for navigating the current complexity in the
world.

Embracing Failure as Feedback:
Change your perspective on failure by viewing it as feedback
rather than a personal flaw. When you encounter setbacks,
analyze what went wrong and why. Use this information to
adjust your strategies and make improvements. By reframing failure as a natural part of the learning process, you'll be
more willing to persevere and take calculated risks in your
endeavors.

14

Prioritize and Reprioritize

As I work to finish this book, I'm feeling swamped. Two failed recruitments for key positions means I'm doing double or triple the work. I've signed a record number of deals, which has led to more design work than usual. Clients have pushed projects back, creating financial pressure, and our international expansion has a significant number of details that need to be addressed. If the additional workload wasn't enough, my daughter is not sleeping well and has a stomach issue.

The more the world bears down, the more I embrace the skill of prioritizing and reprioritizing. As pressure increases, I review my priorities every day. I also reprioritize more than usual and step-up my discipline, so I don't get sidetracked.

With the speed at which the world is moving and changing, the best uses of our attention and time shift daily—sometimes even hourly. Though our primary focus for the quarter may stay the same, the steps we need to take each day and week become fluid. A to-do list for the week helps us stay on track, but by Wednesday, priorities change and the list needs a serious revamp. Rarely does a plan unfold exactly as we envision it. The only solution to the wavering to-do list is prioritization and reprioritization.

Using Prioritization to Maximize Your Resources

Time is a limited resource. We can earn more money and replace material possessions, but after a minute passes, we can't get it back. That's why it's vital to know your purpose and reserve your internal energy for the targets that move you toward your goal.

Professionals today have multifaceted lives. We work, raise families, pursue hobbies, take care of pets, and more. Rarely do we have the luxury of setting and forgetting our priorities. We continually encounter moments when maximizing our impact requires adjusting the dial on how we allocate our focus.

The ability to prioritize and then reprioritize, both individually and organizationally, has become even more essential in the twenty-first century. Schedule shuffling is one of the most obvious adaptations we must make. Without the ability to shift when necessary, our most valuable resource will get used up. It's so easy to get derailed by the tyranny of the urgent, but when we learn to stay focused on our priorities, we find those fires die out or have others who can tend to them.

Almost every client I've spoken with over the past four years has spent the first couple of minutes of our conversation talking about how they're completely underwater. It's a common problem, and doesn't have a ready solution; however, setting priorities and using them to navigate your tasks and schedule will give you a chance to come up for air.

The Art of Subtraction

The new idea of subtraction in the workplace offers promise to corporate executives as well as small business owners, and the beautiful dance of generative AI and other technology breakthroughs bring added resources that allow us to free up time.

Most think more is better. Advertising has convinced us that getting 30% more of anything will change our lives; however, this more philosophy has also cluttered our lives. We sign our children up for every activity and fill each second of our vacations. But successful leaders have begun to see the value of taking things away.

Prioritization means we look at the things that are truly important. Which steps are vital to completing this project? And more pertinent—which ones can we remove? Subtraction gives us permission to simplify and combine efforts. When we first ask those questions that bring reduction, it might feel counter-intuitive, and learning to say no to projects that don't fulfill our mission may seem foolish. However, this tactic will help lighten our loads and prioritize differently. And in the end, it will make us more productive.

As scenarios shift, subtraction may require us to fully abandon some of our initial priorities. Subtraction means becoming comfortable with identifying three priorities for your afternoon then postponing or delegating all of them when something more important comes up. Five valuable subprojects could easily become two as you embrace your capacity and correctly identify those that best fit your purpose.

I find it valuable to set limits with my team concerning the length and subjects of meetings. These boundaries can initially feel awkward or uncomfortable, but the alternative is to lose control of your time, energy, and attention.

Limits and boundaries also allow you to say no. When you prioritize based on your own values and goals, you give yourself permission to turn down other people, goals, or timeframes. Setting and sticking to your priorities clears the clouds and allows you to see the North Star. You can navigate clearly toward your goal.

Reprioritization is a big part of this art of subtraction. We need to become comfortable with not getting to the bottom of our to-do list. The exponential environment we live in means things get added faster than we can finish. With each addition, those who reprioritize give themselves grace and forgiveness. We admit that we may never get to the bottom of the list, and don't feel like a failure because we've succeeded in creating priorities based on our purpose.

Though the learning curve of technology seems to bring chaos, as we master the dance, we will be able to enjoy even more subtraction. Transcription services record our meeting notes, and chatbots take care of basic web customer service. New interactive tools pop up every day, but fortunately, the chaotic speed of the technology may help alleviate some of the turmoil it's causing. And as the new solutions present themselves, the need to prioritize and reprioritize will be even greater.

Perseverance and subtraction work together in a nice paradox, and it's a difficult concept for many over-achievers. Recognizing the difference between persevering toward key priorities and letting go of tasks that have been subjugated by more important projects is an exercise that requires practice, self-awareness, and discipline. Constantly refining this contradictory duo will help you navigate complex and full agendas. You will achieve more by doing less because you'll be aligned with your purpose and less distracted by secondary or unimportant items.

If you are one of the many smart, talented, accomplished people who has difficulty leaving tasks unfinished, I suggest that you ritualize this type of ending. Leave at least one box on your to-do list unchecked every day. Do this consciously and congratulate yourself for your ability to subtract.

The Art of Delegation

I work with many experienced managers who worry about putting too much pressure on their teams. Yes, a good leader helps his or her team avoid overload and burnout, but micromanaging and not delegating is not an effective way of dealing with these issues. By keeping too many tasks for ourselves, we pass on the message that we don't trust the team to be able to prioritize or say no.

When leaders train their teams in the skill sets we've discussed and give them permission to have conversations regarding their workloads and capabilities, we can delegate with confidence, and pass that confidence on to our members.

My team recently coached a senior manager who had been promoted to an executive role. Our client was fully engaged, committed, and extremely operationally competent in her job. Yet, during her first six months, she continually got bogged down in tasks that were not her own. Because she was overly sensitive to any complaint from those who reported to her directly regarding workload or task difficulty, she didn't pass along uncomfortable tasks.

This approach slowed down key strategic projects. It also created tension with her boss, who felt frustrated as the team fell behind on transformation initiatives to help the department keep up with the pace of its growth.

She happily accepted our offer to receive coaching in delegation, assertiveness, and prioritization. She developed new habits, practices, and mindsets. She had a few deep, candid conversations with her boss about consistently revising priorities and developing accountability in her department. These conversations were not necessarily easy or comfortable, but they created trust. Ultimately, the training and conversations have been incredibly powerful and valuable for her, the boss, and the whole team. Movement toward their key strategic goals is now much more fluid. Her team feels motivated as they assume full responsibility for their own work, and she navigates in a much more effective way.

Ritualized Time Management

One impactful aspect of music and dance is the intentional pause. Everything freezes for just a moment. A few in the audience will offer a meager clap because they think the performance might be over; however, before they can put their hands together a second time everything unexpectedly erupts. Similar planned interludes really need to be a part of your calendar.

The best way to navigate change is to use fundamental time management principles as you prioritize your schedule. This includes leaving buffer zones between commitments. Intentional pauses give us the capacity to enjoy the eruption of the next meeting or event. Additionally, they provide space for the unexpected.

By identifying your most important objectives, you can set aside time to focus on them. I recommend developing a ritual to manage your schedule. This is more than a listing of appointments and to-dos—technology gives us many effective options for setting a calendar and collaborating with others. A ritual for time management allows you to go deeper as you check in with yourself, assess how your planned actions align with your vision, and make ongoing adjustments.

For eighteen years, my company has taught time and priority management. Time management has some leeway for personal preference. Some people like to reset their priorities at the end of every week, so they're ready to go the following week. Others prefer a meeting every Monday morning. Either system works if the time spent is focused and productive.

Regardless of your exact system, daily, weekly, monthly, quarterly, and yearly evaluations provide massive benefits. Each allows us to modify our small steps as well as the bigger chunks with clarity and intention. Without planning and follow-up, you won't reach your goal in the timeliest manner. What begins as an overarching plan breaks down into smaller and smaller chunks with each evaluation until we reach the level of micro tasks. A ritualistic style of assessment keeps us productive as we move, modify, or drop tasks as needed every single day. A task that doesn't get completed today moves to tomorrow or next week. Or we may discover it's no longer a priority at all.

Without a ritual, the approach will be haphazard, and important actions will inevitably fall through the cracks. Until we ritualize and deeply embed both the small actions and the overall vision, we won't know where we're going and, as a consequence, won't be able to navigate effectively.

Stay in the Now

Dancing provides a beautiful backdrop to the way we navigate this hectic life. From hip hop to tap to jazz to ballet, each artist must be in the moment. If their thoughts drift to their next move, they'll miss a beat or rush a step. Plus, by being present in the current movement, if someone else in the troupe has a misstep, another member could potentially cover for them. Their priority is now.

When the need to reprioritize comes, we, too, must focus on the present moment. What do I need to do right now to make progress? If we get caught up in what might or should happen in the future, anxiety and a sense of overwhelm will set in.

We need to dream big and set long-term goals, but to achieve them, we have to focus on the step that's before us now. It's important to learn to simultaneously manage and differentiate between short-, medium-, and long-term priorities. Our client, who needed coaching on delegation, is a great example. Until she received support and practiced different skills, she got bogged down with solving immediate problems, at the expense of planning, imagining, and designing new long-term solutions that could ultimately prevent short-term emergencies.

Navigating successfully in this world requires cultivating the capacity to be in flow with what is going on right now, because it allows you to reprioritize efficiently without getting stuck on what you're doing or what could happen down the road.

How Reprioritizing Has Helped Me

As I combine the roles of mother and business owner, prioritizing and reprioritizing rank as my most important skill. Without exaggeration, at least fifty times a day I use this trait to adjust my attention and task list. Moving something forward or back or replacing it entirely is a common occurrence.

Plus, to respect another person's time and conserve my own, I've learned to modify my schedule on the fly. Right in the middle of a conversation, I'll assess my priorities, change plans, and loop in everyone who needs to know about the modification. By ritualizing my priority planning, I can now do it at a moment's notice in sync with the shifting landscape.

Unexpected things happen daily. Children get sick or lose their ride home from school. Your plan to come home, cook dinner, finish answering emails, and relax for a couple minutes gets modified based on what the rest of the family needs. A miserable day or bad grade means you give them a little TLC or review their homework instead of following through on a phone date with a friend or ending your day with a good book.

People often wonder how I keep up with running my own business as a single mother of two kids while traveling for work, organizing birthday parties, and all the rest. My level of high organization means I always know what's on my plate and how I imagine getting it done. With that baseline, I can prioritize and reprioritize much more easily. Knowing the lay of the land and the willingness to adapt allows me to reconfigure and persevere.

In order to navigate in a world with accelerating change and 40,000 unexpected events every day, we must be willing to drop some things from our lists, or at least put them on standby, so you can focus on other things. Effectively prioritizing the path toward your larger vision requires knowing how to prioritize yourself and your team.

People are more important than products. Family ranks above business. Your health and quality of life deserve a high spot on your list of priorities. Adaptation allows us to accelerate as we adjust our schedule and tasks; however, knowing our priorities will send us in the right direction so we can navigate the exponential speed of this digital world.

Genie™ Prompts for Prioritize and Reprioritize

Go to www.talk2genie.com and type in one of these conversation starters:

- Help me with setting my top priorities
- Let's create a daily prioritization routine
- I want to improve my decision-making process
- Create a plan to manage competing priorities
- Build a system for tracking and reviewing priorities
- Let's enhance my ability to reprioritize when needed
- I want to say no to low-priority tasks

Practical Tips to up your game with PRIORITIZE AND REPRIORITIZE.

Make it real, keep it simple, you're a rock star ☺

In today's fast-paced and intricately interconnected world, mastering the art of prioritization and re-prioritization is nothing short of a superpower. It's the key to maintaining your focus on what truly matters amidst the constant whirlwind of demands and opportunities. Here are three practical exercises to empower you with this indispensable skill.

Daily Prioritization:
Start each day by creating a list of your most important tasks or priorities. Be specific about what you want to achieve. Throughout the day, allocate your focus and energy to these tasks before tackling less critical ones. Review your progress regularly and adjust your priorities as needed. This exercise

helps you maintain clarity and concentrate on what truly matters.

Goal Chunking:

Break down your major life objectives into smaller, more manageable tasks or milestones. Create a roadmap or action plan to achieve each of these milestones. By focusing on completing these smaller steps one at a time, you'll maintain clarity and make steady progress toward your larger vision.

Adaptive Goal Setting:

Practice adaptive goal setting by setting both short-term and long-term goals. Short-term goals should be flexible and adjustable to accommodate the changing conditions of a complex and fast-changing environment. Regularly review and adjust your goals as needed based on emerging challenges and opportunities. This exercise will help you stay focused on your objectives while remaining adaptable.

15

Pragmatism

We recently closed a large and strategic project involving several independent clients from a variety of geographical zones. As we moved toward closing, we realized that different elements of our proposal were more attractive to some stakeholders than others. To reach the finish line, we scaled down a few of the options and moved one to a possible second wave of the project.

We knew getting the different stakeholders to align on all points was unlikely. Holding out for them to do so could result in losing the deal altogether. When we presented the modifications, we emphasized that the most important parts of the proposal would remain intact. Although our company would lose some potential revenue by not offering all the possible components, it was a pragmatic way to get the deal signed and into action.

Pragmatic is defined as "dealing with things sensibly and realistically in a way that is based on practical rather than theoretical considerations." Pragmatism is an important skill today because if we give in to overthinking, worrying, or excessive theorizing, we'll miss the boat on important opportunities. Being pragmatic helps us cut through complexity and keep projects on track. Related to subtraction, it allows us to act on our priorities through simplifying and streamlining.

Pursuing a goal is like dancing—you have to move off the sidelines and onto the dance floor to truly enjoy the dance. Form will make it look better, and the more skill you have, the more likely people will stop and take notice. But those who let fear of ridicule and what others think stop them can't succeed. Practicality tells us wallflowers miss the fun.

Paralyzed by Perfectionism

I believe in striving for excellence, and my team and I bring that ethos to our work; however, the extreme will leave you paralyzed by perfectionism. High standards only have feasibility if they don't keep you from navigating forward.

With a perfectionist mindset, we keep fine tuning and adjusting, but we never take it to the dance floor. This is particularly risky in today's fast-moving world because contexts, environments, and objectives change so quickly that by the time you finish perfecting, the opportunity may be over. Pragmatically it's better to take the project to a solid place and then iterate as needed during the early stages. Our best ideas are often the ones that come to us first. So, we should move in confidence with a pragmatic approach.

Seth Godin talked about holding out for perfection. He says, "Any project that's held up in revisions and meetings and general fear-based polishing is the victim of a crime. It's a crime because you're stealing that perfect work from a customer who will benefit from it. You're holding back the good stuff from the people who need it, afraid of what the people who don't will say. Stop polishing and ship instead. Polished perfect isn't better than perfect, it's merely shinier. And late.[22]"

Kary Oberbrunner shares that "holding up a launch because you're afraid of looking foolish, then you're actually harming your future client. You're prideful, because you're focused more on yourself than helping others."[23]

Perfectionism isn't realistic, and it hinders navigation. I have seen countless hours spent trying to convince stakeholders to buy into a project. By the time the last person validates the project, it is irrelevant. In one case, during a major transformation, we worked hard for a client and took multiple trips across France, only to see the general manager leave, and the whole project get canceled.

Harnessing Your Dream

Pragmatism helps you adapt practically and allows you to address multiple competing demands. When we think with a practical mind, we see the places where we're becoming obsessed and losing our way. Pragmatism means revealing the plan before the entire solution is built.

Let's say you have ten steps to achieve your goal. When you reach step two, you realize you're unsure how to complete step three. Give yourself permission to leave it as a question mark until you know more while you dive in and move forward. Often, a simpler prototype will give you a peek into how to complete the project without becoming too bogged down in the theoretical details or elaborate, untested solutions.

Keeping realism and practicality in perspective benefits the whole team. It creates a positive feedback loop, because being pragmatic helps us move forward, and we feel better when we make progress, which reinforces the desire to keep making pragmatic choices.

Dreaming big comes from an emotional place rather than a practical one. It allows your head, heart, and energy to align with a mission that matters to you. When you couple that emotion with the rationality of pragmatism to identify the actions that set you up for the best chance of success, you become unstoppable. Forward progress requires both forces working in tandem.

Emotion gives us energy, and pragmatism channels that energy to help us navigate toward our goals. Without pragmatic focus, you might feel like you're boiling over with undirected anxiety, running in circles instead of toward your goal. Pragmatism lets us harness our passion by applying it in practical ways.

Becoming Pragmatic

Pragmatism, like all the skills we've talked about, can be learned and practiced. You can cultivate it in yourself and your team. When we feel overwhelmed, pragmatism can remind us we don't have to get it all done at once. It shows us how to break the big goal into smaller, more manageable pieces.

When I'm working on a proposal, I go all out. However, the constraints of a deadline and other competing priorities mean I use a pragmatic mindset rather than a perfectionist approach. I'll concede that certain less important slides will come from templates rather than customized creative content. Being okay with reusing content frees me to apply my energy where it will have the greatest impact: on a tailor-made solution for the client.

Learning to define the essentials and take the next step has been a great ally. A comprehensive proposal might be 200 pages long, but no one will read it. A pragmatic approach identifies what brings the greatest value and has the most leverage. Sometimes, scaling your proposal back to two or three main elements and focusing on maximizing their value rather than adding more angles and offerings makes the best impression.

Pragmatically setting your focus can lead to what is sometimes called the minimum viable product (MVP), a stripped-down version of an idea that allows you to launch, test, learn, and iterate, preventing instant obsolescence.

By identifying value and continuously improving instead of waiting for impossible perfection, we can cover massive amounts of ground, despite the ever-accelerating work. If you understand the concepts but still feel overwhelmed, ask yourself whether you're overly theorizing or truly being pragmatic.

How can you slim down what you're trying to do? What would be good enough in this moment to move you a step closer to your objective?

Every prototype needs a certain amount of conceptual planning. However, we also need to recognize when we've gathered enough information to stop thinking and start acting. We learn more about our theories when we engage in them, allowing us to make adjustments as necessary and move forward.

Take Action

The pragmatic approach requires action. The faster the world moves, the more we need to seize the moment and move—not in some frenetic action but running toward the finish line instead of running in place. The goal is to narrow down our concerns to the vital few and then take action more quickly; efficiency is key.

For example, we recently set very firm deadlines to get a buy-in from internal stakeholders faster and get key design elements worked out in the beginning. We engaged ten of 150 business leaders in a pilot session to test key parts of the content and co-build with their feedback. We shared digital documents instead of dealing with the back and forth of PDFs, allowing us to quickly communicate our different perspectives and skillsets. The project—a highly complex leadership program to upskill and align leadership practices with a massive company-wide transformation—is moving forward with remarkable ease. In four weeks, we have done what often takes four months in other contexts.

If you want to move forward, do something. As you act, you'll generate feedback that you can use to navigate. The world will continue to change, new data will become available, and you can adjust as you proceed. That's a pragmatic approach. Pragmatism underpins the ability to collaborate with large numbers of people. Focusing on realism and practicality benefits the whole team. This mindset and approach will help you cut through long conversations and reduce rewrites.

Most people have several concurrent objectives. Achieving them requires pragmatism, which includes prioritizing and reprioritizing. It also helps navigate unanticipated obstacles and make constructive decisions.

A pragmatic approach also relieves stress. When we break our project into practical steps, even when we fall behind, we can see progress. With each completed step, you know you're closer to the goal. It feels good.

Applied Pragmatism

Pragmatism helps navigate every area of life, including choosing where to live or whether to buy a house. I had planned to buy an apartment in 2022, but when the stock market dropped, I decided to wait.

Instead of moving, I decided to get a few fixtures and pieces of furniture for my current place to make it feel fresh and new and take care of some storage issues. Those purchases improved my quality of life, made my current apartment feel cozier, and freed up more space for two growing children, all without derailing my progress.

Addressing a health issue also requires pragmatism. You start by making an appointment with your general practitioner and telling him or your symptoms. That professional might recommend a specialist or testing. By taking practical steps, you can find out what's wrong. Your other option is to theorize and fall down the rabbit hole of WebMD while you worry unnecessarily.

Our business life works the same way. We must come to a practical space between our grandest dream, perfection, and reality. With clients, we may have to compromise to mold their vision into our doable solution. Pragmatism is productive; dogmatism is not. You can maintain your core convictions without making every collaborative decision a battle.

Pragmatism has helped me with our physical office space. We're on the second floor, and over a year ago, a leak on the fifth floor managed to reach our hallway ceiling, which partially caved in. No one was hurt, but a big hole with water leaking from it loomed overhead. Maintenance came and had to puncture a second hole to allow the space to dry out, which he said would take six months.

When the period finally passed, we had just started working with a new office manager. She was just starting to get up to speed on our workflows, projects, and processes. Her arrival and onboarding was putting a strain on the entire team who was trying to keep up with a very busy year.

The ceiling also brought insurance declarations and legal hurdles that needed to be taken care of—things the office manager would normally be responsible for, but were secondary to making sure she got onboarded quickly to key projects. I had to make the conscious decision to be pragmatic and not get annoyed. I decided I would not let seeing the hole in the ceiling be a daily emotional drain on me. We have a beautiful office, and the imperfect hallway did not have to hijack my focus to the detriment of more important concerns. So we let that hole sit for another six months. The office manager dealt with contractors and renovations once she had managed more important priorities. It was a pragmatic approach.

To navigate the most productive route, you must come to terms with imperfection and accept you'll face various headwinds on your journey. By taking steps toward what matters and being practical about letting the rest fall where it will, even when well-meaning people get upset about cosmetic issues, like a hallway ceiling.

Leading with Pragmatism

Successful pragmatics listen to experts rather than allowing emotions to pull them off course. They consult mentors and advisors who've already walked the path they're traversing. Even the most experienced dancers and athletes have coaches. I keep in mind that I ultimately get to make the decision. However, I solicit enough feedback to make an informed and pragmatic decision. Informed decisions allow you to take a strong leadership position because you can cut through the noise and focus on what's most essential to the goal at hand.

When you face less-than-ideal circumstances, you can analyze the situation to identify the greatest points of leverage. No organization can get everything done, and every organization will make mistakes. If you can apply pragmatic, focused leadership, though, you'll have a huge competitive advantage and avoid getting bogged down in the complexity and speed of change.

I periodically think about the proverb that says, "If you're not the doer, don't criticize what the doer's doing." It's easy to theorize, criticize, and complain when things don't go as planned. But pragmatic leaders find the positive. If you take this advice to heart, you will attract pragmatic doers who will help you move toward greater goals.

Genie™ Prompts for Pragmatism

Go to www.talk2genie.com and type in one of these conversation starters:

- Help me with making practical decisions
- Let's create a plan for realistic goal setting
- I want to improve my problem-solving skills
- Create a routine for pragmatic thinking
- Build a strategy for effective time management
- I want to stay focused on practical outcomes
- Help me develop strategies for realistic optimism

Practical Tips to up your game with PRAGMATISM.

Make it real, keep it simple, you're a rock star ☺

In a fast-moving and complex world, the ability to embrace pragmatism is a valuable asset. Pragmatism involves making practical and effective decisions based on the realities of a situation. Here are three simple, practical exercises to help you enhance your pragmatism and navigate this dynamic world with greater ease and effectiveness.

Minimal Viable Product (MVP) Practice:
Embrace the concept of Minimal Viable Product (MVP) development, commonly used in product and project management. When embarking on a new initiative, start by identifying the core features or actions that will achieve the primary goal. Develop and launch the MVP quickly, gathering feedback and making improvements based on practical user insights. This exercise encourages a pragmatic focus on delivering the essential elements first, allowing you to adapt and refine your approach based on real-world feedback rather than hypothetical scenarios, making your endeavors more efficient and effective.

SWOT Analysis for Decision-Making:
Incorporate SWOT (Strengths, Weaknesses, Opportunities, Threats) analysis into your decision-making process. Before making important choices, conduct a thorough SWOT analysis for each option or scenario. Identify the internal strengths and weaknesses as well as external opportunities and threats associated with each choice. This exercise encourages a pragmatic approach by ensuring you consider both internal capabilities and external factors when making decisions, ultimately leading to more informed and practical choices.

Prioritization Impact Analysis:
When managing your tasks and projects, implement a prioritization impact analysis. Assess the potential impact and consequences of each task or project in relation to your goals and the broader context. Prioritize those that offer the most significant impact with the least amount of resources or effort. This exercise encourages you to align your actions with practical objectives, ensuring you invest your time and resources where they can make the most substantial difference.

16

Collaboration

My son and two other students have been working on a project about Egypt for school, and I've been collaborating with the other parents to support the kids' success. One set of adults took them to see an Egyptian exhibit at the Louvre, and we've all taken turns hosting them in our homes. Collaborating with these parents increased my feeling of connection to the school community. My son and I both feel fulfilled in these partnerships.

Collaboration has been bringing people together for centuries. Kings used arranged marriages to unite nations, allied troops won wars, Tchaikovsky and Marius Petipa brought their talents together to give us the Nutcracker and Rogers and Hammerstein have created beauty and brought people together in droves to experience their masterpieces.

And even though we've learned to work in remote offices, collaboration is still a hugely powerful navigational force in today's fast-moving, chaotic, and often disconnected world. By collaborating, we can work more efficiently and more reliably identify and take the next step in the dance of work and life.

When you watch a couple waltz or a dance troupe move in harmony, you can see the value of collaboration. The dancers have a keen sense of each other's movements, and they work closely together—physically, mentally, and emotionally—to create beauty and fluidity. That deep connection comes through hours and years of practice, followed by being completely present in the performance.

Further Together

Perhaps you've heard the phrase, "Alone, you can go faster, but together, you can go further." Without collaboration, you risk limiting the reach of your impact. The stakes are high in the modern economy, and if you don't reach outside of your sphere to collaborate, you can quickly become obsolete. Technology, markets, and competition are moving too quickly to keep up all by yourself.

My company continually experiments and collaborates with different tech companies to innovate and stay on the cutting-edge. Recently, we created the Love Triangle™. It's an experimentation framework that allows us to innovate and try out new ideas in a collaborative environment with clients. The triangle represents three parties: The client as the final user, my company as the expert in soft skills, and a new technology or learning method as the novelty. Experimentation and innovation come to life through the collaboration between these three entities. It allows us to quickly test new learning solutions to see if they are effective.

Given the pace of the world, if you don't move swiftly toward your goal, someone else will beat you there. But as we previously discussed, we aim to hit a moving target. Not only do you need to go fast, you also need to go far. Strategic partnerships determine the level of your success. Your capacity to exist comfortably in the paradoxes of short and long term thinking and planning is also crucial.

On those days when you get stuck in your own head or ideas don't come, collaboration offers sounding boards and innovation. It also offers constructive debate as people who come at current problems from a completely different perspective challenge your projects and ask questions you'd not thought of.

Collaboration brings diversity to the table. With so many ideas and options, we'll be forced to weigh the pros and cons and meld innovations. The key to navigating to the goal line is never getting so married to your part of the idea that you can't let go when your collaborators begin to make it unrecognizable. We go further when we can release our melody line and let the harmony rise to the forefront.

For instance, we have an exercise we used with our coaches in preparation for launching a summit focused entirely on adaptability. We were collaborating with a new partner who offers a surprising and intense virtual reality exercise, and we were looking at different ways to integrate it into our programs. Eleven coaches split into four different teams and then brainstormed ways to build a program incorporating the module. In an hour and a half, the group created four different programs.

To push it even further, we decided to meet again two weeks later and come up with four entirely new ideas, forbidding ourselves to use any of the materials we generated the first time. By collaborating, setting new parameters, and collaborating again, we upped the ante and generated even more creative, diverse solutions.

If I had been forced to develop even one program on my own, it would have been easy to get stuck in my own thoughts. I would have needed to imagine all the people who would use it. Conversely, in a collaboration, people constantly chime in to ask, "What if we put this there? What do you think about this addition? Could we try this way?" The whole process becomes a dynamic, living, creative exercise with the ability to achieve a greater level of depth in the most efficient manner. Maybe I could jam something out more quickly on my own, but it wouldn't be as rich.

You can try to do everything yourself, but I believe it takes a village to run a business and to succeed in today's world in general. We need others to help fill the gaps in our expertise. Some important issues never occur to us because we've never experienced them while other people know them intimately.

Practical Collaborations

A few years ago, our company created an innovative digital learning platform. The building process was highly complex. We're not tech specialists, so we formed partnerships with different tech companies. Their complementary perspective and knowledge base opened doors to areas that were completely out of reach before. Our impact grew by giant leaps, and our work had much greater depth and breadth.

In today's world, you don't have to build technology or do it all. In fact, the attempt might slow you down to the point that your idea becomes obsolete before you can make it a reality. If you're not on the cutting edge, it's easy to bite off more than you can chew. Going solo can lead to results that fall short of your vision. The future of business lies in figuring out who you can partner with, not what you can invent on your own.

On multiple occasions, our big tech clients have partnered with some of their own clients—or even their competitors. The same is true in my business. A few years ago, you might never have considered partnering with a competitor, but now such a collaboration can represent a strong strategic move. Combining forces allows you to leverage your strengths while they fill in your weaknesses, and vice versa, unleashing enormous potential and new ideas you never would have come up with otherwise.

For example, the virtual reality we incorporated into our program was created by a competitor. We sell similar services but wanted to harness this incredibly powerful and specific tool they created that helps people identify how they react under pressure. Some clients report they feel like they've undergone ten years of coaching in three minutes because they learn so much about themselves.

We're also collaborating with a client who has access to a group of people to train. We, in turn, have the know-how regarding training and coaching. One collaboration can lead to another, opening more and more doors and expanding your scope. If you only work with your own material, skill sets, and assets, you limit yourself. Instead of trying to do everything on your own, collaborations bring the necessary ingredients together much faster and more fully. Collaborative partnerships are key to succeeding in today's world, especially when the ground is constantly shifting beneath your feet.

Finding Support in Collaboration

Collaboration also incorporates the element of support. Sometimes a dose of collaboration can help get you over the hump. It can be as simple as reaching out for advice or a sounding board, even if you go back to working on the problem yourself.

Often, simply outlining a problem to someone gives me newfound inspiration. Other times, when I'm not sure what I think or how to make up my mind, it's helpful to hear what a trusted confidant would do. Whenever I face a large personal decision, I reach out to at least a handful of people who play different roles in my life and come from different backgrounds. Questioning others has served me extremely well.

When you solicit others' input to enrich your own decision-making, you may be surprised by the responses. Sometimes I think I'm overreacting, but a friend will validate my response. I also get new ideas about how to manage problems.

Having a conversation doesn't mean you have to take the advice you get. Sometimes advice that doesn't fit your situation helps clarify what you will work instead. Friends have teased me for asking for advice then not taking it. From my perspective, that advice matures my own decision-making process. Even if I don't adopt their solution, hearing it helps formulate my perspective and shows me where to go next. Asking for advice doesn't mean having to accept it without modification.

Being Part of the Collective

The beauty of collaboration lies in being part of a collective rather than working in isolation. Our very survival requires us to let go of ego and consider what's best for everyone moving forward.

My team continually talks about co-elevation, co-creation, and co-construction. We use many "co-" words because we have a concrete sense that through this connection, we will overcome the challenges the world faces. Individualistic behavior simply won't cut it. When you're in a collaborative mindset, you can connect to greater energy. People feel better in connection.

Today, we're connected to the rest of the world in a way like never before—through social media, the internet, rapid modes of transit, and seamless communication. With the click of a button, you can find others who have the skills and attributes you need to complete your ideas. This high level of sharing gives us ever-increasing collaborations.

Consider the number of wikis available today. Wikipedia develops at a rate of two edits per second. [24] WikiTree has brought genealogists from around the world together. WikiTravel, WikiHow, and Wiktionary are only a few of the countless web pages that invite worldwide collaboration to share knowledge and increase awareness.

We're evolving to be more and more collaborative, and if we harness that tendency for good, we can tackle giant problems as a community.

Strengthening our focus on collaboration will put us on the path to solving our greatest societal challenges and bring us a better tomorrow.

Collaboration shows that one plus one often equals more than two. Working together has a multiplicative effect in progressing toward big goals, and some of the outcomes of collaboration are more significant and meaningful than we'd ever expect. By coming together, we learn and grow more as part of a collective than we ever could on our own.

Genie™ Prompts for Collaboration

Go to www.talk2genie.com and type in one of these conversation starters:

- Help me improve my teamwork skills
- Let's create a plan for effective collaboration
- I want to build trust with my team
- Create a strategy for managing team conflicts
- Build a network of collaborative partners
- Enhance my ability to contribute to team projects
- I want to foster a collaborative environment

Practical Tips to up your game with COLLABORATION.

Make it real, keep it simple, you're a rock star ☺

In today's whirlwind of a fast-moving and intricately woven world, the ability to collaborate harmoniously is nothing short of a navigational beacon guiding individuals and teams toward the achievement of shared objectives. Below, you'll discover three immersive practical exercises designed to empower you with the art of collaboration, helping you chart a course through this dynamic landscape with even greater effectiveness.

Networking and Collaborative Partnerships:
Expand your professional network and seek collaborative partnerships with individuals and organizations in related or complementary fields. Attend industry conferences, join online forums, and engage in networking events to build valuable connections. Collaborative partnerships can provide access to new resources, insights, and market opportunities,

bolstering your competitive advantage in a fast-changing, complex world.

Innovation Hackathons:
Organize innovation hackathons or ideation events within your organization or community. Invite participants from various backgrounds and expertise areas to form teams and tackle specific challenges or projects within a limited timeframe, typically ranging from a few hours to a few days. These intense collaborative sessions push teams to think creatively, develop prototypes, and present solutions. Hackathons encourage cross-functional collaboration, rapid ideation, and problem-solving, making them an ideal exercise for fostering both innovation and effective teamwork in a fast-moving and complex world.

Volunteer and Community Engagement:
Get involved in volunteer work and community engagement initiatives. Collaborating with diverse groups of people on community projects not only benefits your local area but also sharpens your collaboration skills. You'll learn to work alongside individuals from different backgrounds, with varying perspectives and priorities, towards a common cause. Volunteering encourages adaptability, empathy, and a shared sense of purpose—attributes that are invaluable when navigating complex and rapidly changing environments. Additionally, community engagement strengthens your bonds with others, creating a network of potential collaborators and allies in your endeavors.

17

Learning and Growing

In nearly every chapter so far, I've mentioned the need for continually learning and growing. In a world changing as speedily as ours, without a lifelong learning mindset, you'll get left behind.

Imagine the energy in the hall on the night of the dance studio's recital. Parents, grandparents, aunts, uncles, and friends gather to watch the budding talent. When the three-year-olds take the stage, smiles abound. Even if the wee ones are total strangers, everyone enjoys watching their antics. The tutus are adorable, but there is no rhythm or unity to speak of. Still, the audience gives the tiny group a hearty round of applause.

Later in the evening, the curtain rises on young ladies—sixteen-year-olds who've been dancing since they turned three. Each hair in place, costumes steamed to perfection, their lyrical movements and graceful steps take your breath away. They synchronize flawlessly, and every motion brings the music to life right before your eyes.

The more excellent of these older students may see a standing ovation when they finish. But without the advancement of their technique and the extra choreography they've learned, we wouldn't hear more than a gratuitous handclap or two. Dancing with grace requires learning new moves, forms, and steps. Similarly, dancing with chaos requires the growth that comes with learning and unlearning—learning the skills we've outlined so far, and unlearning things that may have been useful in the past but are no longer applicable.

The Risks of Not Learning and Growing

Learning and growing are foundational to every endeavor, and while they may seem to be rooting skills, with each piece of information we add to our arsenal, we can navigate more clearly and keep up with life's exponential changes. Some say you're either growing or dying, and in business, this means you're either expanding or shrinking. The only other option is death.

I've been coaching and training since 2005, so obviously, I have a passion for continual learning. We can see the effects of a lack of education all around the world. Illiteracy causes higher death rates and shorter lifespans. Even in the United States, lack of education has a direct correlation to poor health. [25] Mothers in foreign countries have unsuspectingly signed their children over to traffickers because they couldn't read the paper they were signing. These mothers trusted that their children would be sponsored by an American family to get a good education and then be returned with the promise of a bright future. The most basic education would have saved these families great heartache. [26]

While the risks of refusing to grow might not be so dire for business owners, the likelihood of undesirable consequences are just as high. *Entrepreneur Magazine* says, "Companies that don't grow won't survive . . . Without growth fueling those fires of success, your company may not last long." They go on to say that growth means faster cash flows.

Too many of the negative movements and undercurrents of society stem from ignorance. And unfortunately, not a few of the millions of bits of data added every day contribute. Education helps us avoid succumbing to the growing problem of propaganda and malicious influence by charismatic but ill-intentioned leaders. Without a learning and growth mindset, people risk getting caught up in dangerous scams or otherwise being taken advantage of.

Without learning, growing, and challenging ourselves to co-elevate, we put ourselves at risk of large-scale negative forces in the world, socially, ecologically, and militarily. Our world could easily spin out of control, so learning and growth represent a form of risk management.

On one hand, we have so much potential. We could cure cancer and every other horrible disease. We could prolong people's lifespans by hundreds of years. We could solve world hunger. On the other hand, a bioterrorism attack could wipe out the entire planet, we could fail to address climate change and make the planet unlivable, or we could let democracy fall to dictators. If you are not actively doing your part to co-elevate through learning and growth, you are doing a disservice to the world.

The Means of Learning and Growing

Growth and learning happen together. One promotes the other in a beautiful cycle. But learning that produces growth is more than just gathering information. It means developing new behaviors, mindsets, and skills and applying them to your life.

Some learn better by hearing or watching, while others need to touch or act. Information that leads to new behaviors and mindsets usually comes with an emotional attachment. Anytime the idea holds importance or offers some reward, it becomes easier to learn. Regardless, with repetition, we can learn almost anything.

Those behaviors, mindsets, and communication practices are the soft skills my company specializes in. When people engage with the tools we offer, I see them learning and growing right before my eyes. Soft skills require concrete practice—it's not enough for me to tell someone the concepts or explain the theory behind the methodology and send them out the door. They need to practice in a supportive setting with the aid of a coach and then experiment with applying them in the context of their professional lives.

Recently, one senior-level executive, despite their wealth of experience, needed training and coaching on connecting soft skills to their daily practice to help them recharge and navigate in a transformative working environment. In a more straightforward, linear scenario, they had maneuvered fine, but now they needed support to level up in a complex, fast-moving, continually changing organization.

Their new environment required a retooling of their existing skills, as well as learning and growth to deepen their understanding. They discovered new ways to field the chaos of day-to-day demands while keeping their higher purpose and longer-term objectives in sight. Part of the strategy involved figuring out how to cultivate more autonomy in their team, to minimize the need for managerial guidance so the leaders could keep their head above water.

Cultivating these skills in yourself as a leader allows you to teach and coach the people you lead, so they can become more effective, self-sufficient, and resilient, magnifying their and your impact, individually and collaboratively. Soft skills aren't actually "soft" at all. Though they're behavioral, they're concrete and measurable.

The Beautiful Cycle of Learning and Growing

Learning is the intake; growth is the output. When we grow, we handle challenges more effectively, solve problems more quickly, take on more responsibility, and have a larger impact. The growth process expands us and offers value in its application. There is joy, peace, and serenity in this self-perpetuating cycle.

Growth also needs to be in sync with your objectives. Compared to even a decade ago, jobs today have changed dramatically. You could be in the same industry doing a similar job, but the way you do it and the required skills have transformed. This kind of change isn't going away. If you want to be able to navigate the pace of acceleration, you will need to become a more adept learner and stay open to continuous improvement.

Often, we grow in the process of trying to achieve an objective. Whether or not we reach it—it's the effort that drives growth. When you push yourself outside your comfort zone—the things you're used to, comfortable with, and proficient at—you grow.

Growth also occurs when major, unexpected events happen. Even negative experiences full of adversity offer opportunities to choose how to react. Growth means that you rise to the occasion, an expression that captures the expansion involved in growth. You're still in the same body, but you become bigger.

Growth brings transcendence, which can give you a sense of serenity and peace. It helps you break through the physical limits of time and space. It's your brain and your body, but there's no limit to what you can learn or how much you can grow.

The rapidly changing world demands that we constantly learn, unlearn, and grow. Job requirements change almost daily, as do strategies for managing organizations. Learning the soft skills in this book—and unlearning habits that no longer serve you—is foundational to personal and professional growth in the technological age.

Part of learning means constantly refreshing and strengthening our skillsets. You need a whole range of tools because you never know which one or which combination you'll need to pull out in a given moment. You can prepare for that uncertainty by constantly nourishing the desire to learn.

When you consciously feed your appetite for learning, it builds on itself. Traveling to one foreign country stokes the desire to travel to another one. Mastering one skill inspires us to apply it in a new context or master another skill. Once you've opened the door to lifelong learning and growing, you'll find it one of the greatest channels to enjoying this world with less resistance and overwhelm.

This mindset of constant development deeply connects you to appreciating and dancing with the current rhythm of the world. The more you learn and grow, the easier it will be for you to take on the multifaceted, unforeseen, rapid changes that arise. Focusing on learning and growth is one of the best antidotes to feeling exhausted, overwhelmed, frustrated, and tired because it cultivates a sense of serenity amid the complexity.

Different ways of learning work for different people. Some grow best with a coach. Others learn from documentaries, books, and technology. Meditating and yoga can help you clear your mind to make room for new ideas, and musical instruments or new physical activities can stretch you, which opens the door to even more learning.

Spreading the Desire to Learn and Grow

Learning and growth will help you achieve your short-, medium-, and long-term goals. If you're not learning and growing, then you're going backward. Cultivating a mindset that values learning and growth is like having taste buds to enjoy awesome food. It's extraordinarily fulfilling, pleasurable, and enjoyable. Take advantage of that gift.

It's also not just about you. Today's world relies on interconnection. Everyone needs to engage with change to different degrees because the stakes are high and require adaptation and evolution. In learning and growing, you become a model for others, promoting the co-elevation so essential to saving our world. We all influence the people around us. Those who look up to and admire you will see your thirst for learning and commitment to growing. As a result, you'll play a part in a larger story of spreading positive behavior through your community and the world.

One of my core values is ensuring that my children see, hear, and talk about learning and growth. They regularly watch me soaking up new things. We have a culture of continual improvement. I model that behavior and name it so they can apply it to their lives and keep passing it along in a positive feedback loop.

Lifelong learning is not just a Human Resources catchphrase. It's spreading in personal and professional networks for the right reasons. We should promote it as an organically growing trend. If I model it for my children and colleagues, they will, in turn, model it for the people they know. You can do the same in your own network, and together, we can help expand this force of positivity in the world.

Genie™ Prompts for Learning and Growing

Go to www.talk2genie.com and type in one of these conversation starters:

- Help me identify my learning goals
- Let's create a personal development plan
- I want to build a habit of continuous learning
- Create a routine for skill development
- Build a network for learning and growth
- Let's reflect on my learning experiences
- I want to overcome learning challenges

Practical Tips to up your game with LEARNING AND GROWING.

Make it real, keep it simple, you're a rock star ☺

In our contemporary, rapidly changing world, the pursuit of continuous learning and personal growth has become not just an option, but a necessity for remaining both relevant and highly effective. Below, you'll discover three practical exercises crafted to empower you in your journey toward enhanced learning and growth. These exercises equip you with the tools needed to traverse the ever-shifting landscape of our dynamic world with heightened ease and effectiveness.

Read Wider Challenge:
Challenge yourself to read regularly and diversify your reading material (or video material if you prefer to watch or listen than to read). Set a goal to read a certain number of books, articles,

or research papers each month. Choose topics that expand your knowledge and interests, including subjects outside your comfort zone. This exercise encourages intellectual curiosity and a habit of lifelong learning. By regularly exposing yourself to new ideas and perspectives, you'll stay adaptable and well-informed in a world where knowledge is constantly evolving.

Mentorship and Reverse Mentorship:
Seek mentorship from individuals who possess expertise or have had experiences that you admire or want to learn from. Additionally, consider engaging in reverse mentorship, where you mentor someone from a different generation or background. Mentorship provides opportunities for mutual learning and growth. Your mentor can offer valuable guidance and insights, while reverse mentorship allows you to gain fresh perspectives and insights from mentees. This dual approach to mentorship fosters personal growth, adaptability, and a deeper understanding of diverse viewpoints in our ever-evolving world.

Skill Challenges for Continuous Growth:
Embrace the power of skill-specific challenges or projects as a dynamic avenue for honing your abilities and nurturing personal growth. Whether you're an aspiring graphic designer or a seasoned coder, tailor your challenges to your area of expertise. For instance, if you're a graphic designer, immerse yourself in the task of crafting a fresh design every single day for an entire month. These skill challenges not only furnish you with structured opportunities for deliberate practice but also serve as fertile ground for experimentation and innovation within your chosen domain. By consistently embracing such challenges, you'll not only refine your skills but also foster a spirit of perpetual learning and self-improvement— indispensable traits for thriving in our ever-evolving world.

18

Slowing Down

I n every dance or musical performance, the program includes
a variety of pieces designed to give the audience a moving
experience. After movements that include spins and leaps,
as well as rapid beats and driving crescendos, the maestro will
strategically insert a pause—a momentary break in the music
or a slow piece to prepare you for the next rise in the performance. In order to navigate effectively and dance in the
chaos, we need just such a rest.

Throughout the book, I've talked about how this multifaceted world is quickly changing. The different dimensions
intersect, creating complexity and chaos. After all this talk of
acceleration and keeping up, you might assume I'm arguing
for you to speed up. In truth, I want to help you cultivate
these skills so you have the resources you need to slow down.

In this world full of roller-coaster-style movement, systems that force you to decelerate, think clearly, and stop your internal movement are essential. A coach wisely told me that in order to go fast, you have to go slow. Understanding that paradox allows you to breathe, take appropriate breaks, and find a productive rather than frenetic space.

Slowing Down Helps Us Speed Up

The modern world can be overwhelming. Success requires developing skills that allow you to proceed with intention rather than speed. Some decisions require longer, deeper thought. Some problems need to be researched. Maybe you need a vacation or permission to disconnect from email for a week.

Slowing down can mean giving yourself a break from your regular day-to-day or taking time to focus a bit more deeply. It usually means making room to listen—to yourself, your team, or your family. You might simply need a cup of coffee in the middle of the morning to adequately discuss something important to you instead of jumping from topic to topic without achieving your aims.

Some people take a step back by going to see a movie, lying on the beach, or finding another moment of relaxation and leisure without the expectation of a certain result. While other people just need to reduce their number of projects from ten to three.

More than creating a space in time, slowing down involves a deliberate action preempted by clarity and intention rather than a frantic reaction.

Imagine driving a car in a torrential downpour. Are you the kind of person who slows down, pulls off the road, or speeds through hydroplaning all over the place? Most of us think that third option is dangerous. Still, many people live their lives in just such a way.

Everything moves so fast, sometimes it's difficult to see where we're going. Slowing down helps us navigate through the rough patches and see the road ahead a bit more clearly. If you can't slow down in your work and home life, it could end up just as catastrophic as your tires losing connection with the pavement.

Yes, there will still be times when we need to stay focused and move fast. Like the person who drives the fire truck or the ambulance or a running back trying to advance in the game. However, if we're constantly in that high energy fight mode, we'll soon burn out. Downshifting changes the way we breathe, it widens our perspective and even allows our brain to get more oxygen. Studies show that taking a big inhale before a cognitive activity tends to improve performance. [27]

Slowing Down to Increase the Learning Curve

If you never take the time to take a step back, you won't adequately be able to see your own accomplishments. Plus, you'll overlook the more subtle changes in our fast-paced world and miss an opportunity to adapt.

Slowing down as we learn a new skill is essential. Consider those times you've attempted to teach a child to swing a tennis racket, write their letters, or bead a necklace. They initially want to do it as fast and as well as their instructor, but this leads to frustration, and it actually inhibits their ability to learn the task. On the other hand, teachers who slow down their movements or break the lesson into smaller pieces give children permission to take their time and concentrate on mimicking the slow motion. Inevitably, they pick up the new skill rather quickly.

When my daughter began to learn to bead, she thought she would never develop the speed and dexterity I have; however, after practicing at a slow even pace just ten times, she can now create beautiful jewelry with ease.

Slowing down bolsters our capacity to learn. It gives us space to memorize new information and creates more accuracy in the long run. All the micro-gestures of the slow motion learning come together as you accelerate.

Consider our concept of dance. When even the most polished professional learns new choreography, they go through it step by step. Often there will be no music, just the rhythmic count of the instructor. The first few rehearsals take it slower than the final tempo. But as each motif is conquered, the troupe accelerates until they can finally navigate the entire piece with an orchestra. What began as an exercise in discipline becomes a thing of beauty.

Pacing Yourself

As with every skill, some come by them more naturally than others. Fortunately, slowing down can be as simple as carving out time in your schedule. This often means just using your calendar to prioritize specific times so you can be fully present and gain new perspective.

Slowing down must be intentional, and sometimes it's best done with rituals. These may change over time; however, identifying and committing to moments of rest and calm allows you to keep your higher purpose in your sights. Some people use meditation, others schedule daily intervals to read or enjoy nature.

I take a few international flights each year, traveling between homes. These offer tremendous, albeit forced, opportunities to slow down. The Paris to Miami trip gives me ten hours to decompress, unplug from WiFi, and let go.

Each of the skills I've mentioned requires continual practice and helps define how I organize my schedule. Some days involve moving forward and more intense, high-energy bursts. But I also have to make time to clean up, delegate, explain, and tie up loose ends. The most difficult days for entrepreneurs to schedule for themselves is free time.

Our businesses constantly need our attention, and if you love what you do, you might not even notice how much or how hard you are working. Regardless, cutting the bonds and slowing down from time to time is imperative.

My children and I usually engage in one lazy morning each weekend. We enjoy having a day without the normal rush to get dressed and out the door. While everyone should enjoy a guilt free lazy day every now and then, they are especially precious when you have kids at home.

Whatever strategy you use, engineer those slow-down moments. When I'm in Miami, I take advantage of the time difference. By afternoon in Florida, the business day in Paris has ended. I can then schedule free time or work on projects that require deeper, uninterrupted thought.

Too often, we find ourselves running in ten directions at once. Why do we refuse to indulge ourselves in that luxury of slowing down? In truth, we end up having more energy when we give ourselves some breathing room. "Stop and smell the roses" may be an old cliché; however, the concept is vital if we want to be able to enjoy the dance in this chaotic world.

If we don't cultivate a practice of intentionally slowing down, the world will suck us into the vortex of its velocity. The most ambitious might find themselves underwater for years at a time.

In addition to free days, we need free moments. As I mentioned above, some use meditation, while others journal or simply stop for a quiet cup of coffee. I like to take the time to stretch for ten minutes each morning before my children wake. I focus on my movements and clear my head. It helps with circulation and keeps me limber. Plus, the practice roots my mind, so I start the day in a better place.

Our partner, AQai, begins every meeting with a practice of positive focus. At first, I felt antsy and wanted to get on with business. It's nice to hear everyone's positives, but it seemed separate from the real work. In time, though, I realized the practice not only brings everyone into a positive energy space, which is important, but it also makes everyone slow down. After rushing into a meeting, participants get a few minutes to become present. You reap the benefit of being more positive and grounded, and the moments you spend on the practice ultimately make the core content of the meeting go faster.

Slow Down for the People You Love

I recently carved out a memorable slow-down evening with my daughter, Marianna. It was the end of a long, intense week for both of us. With James at camp in the northeast, she had experienced her first week of American day camp, and unlike her French school, she didn't have nap time. By Friday, she was a cranky, hot mess.

Meanwhile, I was juggling the time difference between me and my clients as well as the whole French world being in that mad rush to get projects tied up before vacations begin. Both my five-year-old daughter and my forty-year-old self were going into the weekend tired and electrified—not in a good way.

On Saturday evening. I said, "Let's go to the movies and see *The Minions*." She thought that sounded great. We got all dressed up and took an Uber to the theater.

We were so in the moment that, for a time, nothing else existed. Sometimes you can create these moments, and sometimes they just happen. The night could have been chaotic and tantrum-filled. I could have gotten annoyed with someone in the movie theater. There were a million ways for it to go wrong, but this simple activity ended up being special because we slowed down.

We didn't invent anything new, but the experience felt meaningful from beginning to end. She thought it was fun to buy movie tickets from a kiosk and press the buttons. Even ordering popcorn was exciting. The movie itself was hilarious. Afterward, we took pictures with the characters and then walked in the hot, balmy Miami night to get ice cream. Marianna stopped to dance with a Transformer statue we found, and we enjoyed an unhurried, somewhat unchoreographed evening full of memories.

Sending proposals and returning phone calls never crossed my mind, and I didn't think about the dishes we left in the sink. We simply enjoyed each other and the moment. It might sound trivial or silly, but taking a five-year-old out for a movie and ice cream gave me energy and a sense of magic that I loved. That's what slowing down does: it energizes in a positive, peaceful, serene way for a long time.

Slow Down for Yourself

At the end of the day, mastering the ins and the outs of this particular period of transition and transformation we're living through comes back to some basic truths, such as needing to enjoy life. My whole point in writing is to help you learn to dance, and let's face it, dancing should be fun.

Surely, you've danced with the person of your dreams and had that magical feeling or spent an evening with friends moving at least awkwardly on a crowded dance floor. Fortunately, dancing doesn't have to always be pretty, but it should make us laugh or leave us with fun memories. Without that magical feeling or sense of joy, what's the point? Why learn the dance if you can't have fun?

Perhaps you don't like to dance. Well, dancing with chaos isn't optional. Everyone gets on the dance floor, but if we learn the moves, we don't get jerked around by the crowd, and we'll trip over our own feet less.

Slowing down helps combat feelings of overwhelm. For instance, a friend of mine recently finalized a divorce, but many other things were in motion in her life too. Turning forty, traveling the world, and looking for apartments were just the prelude to the dance. She'd planned to move a short distance but then decided to relocate out of state. The first apartment she found seemed great, but grabbing it before someone else signed the lease put pressure on her. She hadn't yet wrapped up her travels, and a trip to visit family and reunite with her college sweetheart were on the table, too.

She decided to slow down and reprioritize. After much deliberation, she reached some grounding decisions that left her feeling secure and confident.

Slowing down has the potential to give us tremendous clarity about the things we find most important—personally, professionally, as a citizen of your community, and of the world. Creating slow-down moments generates meaning and a life worth living. All the skills in this book come from the collaborative spirit of co-elevation and joy. The faster the world moves, the more important it is to carve out times to slow down.

Genie™ Prompts for Slowing Down

Go to www.talk2genie.com and type in one of these conversation starters:

- Help me develop a daily mindfulness practice
- Let's create a routine for unwinding after work
- I want to learn how to prioritize self-care
- Create a plan for reducing stress
- Build a habit of digital detox
- Let's enhance my ability to enjoy quiet moments
- I want to be more present in the moment

Practical Tips to up your game with SLOWING DOWN.

Make it real, keep it simple, you're a rock star ☺

Amidst the hustle and intricacies of today's interconnected world, mastering the art of slowing down emerges as an invaluable skill, one that not only enriches personal well-being but also supercharges effectiveness. Below, discover three meticulously crafted practical exercises to nurture this skill, empowering you to gracefully navigate the swift currents and intricate pathways of our fast-paced and complex world, all while maintaining your sense of calm and enhancing your efficacy.

Nature Immersion:
Spend time in nature by immersing yourself in outdoor environments. Activities like Forest Bathing involve mindful and intentional walks through natural settings and focusing on the sensory experiences of the forest. Engage your senses by observing the sights, sounds, smells, and textures of the natural

world, whether you are in remote settings or a city park. This practice promotes relaxation, reduces stress, and encourages a profound sense of connection to the natural environment. Regular nature immersion sessions provide a powerful antidote to the fast pace of our intense lifestyles, allowing you to slow down and appreciate the present moment.

A Day Without Rushing:
The objective of this exercise is to experience an entire day without rushing, embracing a slower, more deliberate pace of life. Begin your day by setting a clear intention to move through the day without rushing. Remind yourself that the goal is not to accomplish more tasks but to savor each moment. Start your morning with a few minutes of mindfulness meditation to visualize a calm day ahead. During breakfast, eat mindfully. Throughout the day, perform tasks with deliberation and focus on one thing at a time. Schedule short breaks for reflection and relaxation. Unplug from digital devices during meals. Spend time in nature if possible. In the evening, reflect on your day and consider making this practice a regular part of your routine to appreciate the richness of each experience and reduce stress.

Slow Travel and Exploration:
Whether you're embarking on a journey to a far-flung foreign destination or taking a short trip to the village next door, you will love this one! The goal is to cultivate a profound connection with the places you encounter, fostering a deeper appreciation for their unique charm and cultural diversity.

Choose your destination thoughtfully, considering whether it's near or far, and prepare to immerse yourself in the local culture. Engage wholeheartedly with the residents, take part in their traditions, and savor the local cuisine to fully experience the essence of the place.

Instead of rushing from one site to another, embrace a leisurely pace of exploration, allowing yourself to meander through markets, streets, and hidden corners. Absorb the sights, sounds, and scents of your surroundings, capturing moments through photography as memories to cherish.

Connect genuinely with the local community, seeking out conversations that provide insights into their lives and perspectives. Appreciate the diversity of the world, recognizing that each place possesses its own unique allure and cultural richness.

After your journey, take time to reflect on the experiences that left a lasting impact and share these stories with others to spread awareness and inspire an appreciation for the world's diverse cultures and landscapes near and far.

By embracing the principles of slow travel and mindful exploration, this exercise allows you to savor the richness of your experiences and develop a profound connection with the global community and yourself, no matter where your journey takes you.

PART FOUR
Let Yourself Dance

19

Embracing the Chaos

chaotic world isn't new; however, the twenty-first century seems to be spinning faster than any time period before. Artificial intelligence continually finds ways to take over the most mundane tasks. Technology allows us to work states and continents away from others in our organization, and work we accomplish today could very well be irrelevant tomorrow. We cannot change these facts. Our only alternative to survive in this exponential turmoil is to embrace it, leverage it, and learn to dance with it.

Similar to the tempo of the music when we're on the dance floor, the orchestra or the DJ controls the playlist. We don't know what the next rhythm will sound like, but we can change our steps to accommodate the current song.

Our dance with chaos begins with the eighteen soft skills we've talked about in this book. Because while we can't change the speed at which robotics and AI transform the world, we can change our skill set.

Start Where You Are

The ever-changing environment offers potential for advancement as well as decline. Prior to the pandemic, World Vision reported tremendous progress in reducing world hunger. [28] Though that crisis did cause a setback, thanks to technology helping spread the news and the number of world service agencies investing in this global problem, more families get help every day. Unfortunately, the same technology gives rise to cyber-crime like bullying and criminals reaching into pockets a world away.

We could focus on the negative forces in this chaotic world, but that won't change anything. To maximize our possibilities, we must acknowledge and accept these evil forces, but we don't have to dance with them. By choosing our dance partner, we have the power to embrace the positive and make a larger impact than anyone fifty years ago imagined–anyone except Edward Lorenz.

In the 1960s, Edward Lorenz left his computer to get a cup of coffee. The meteorological simulations he'd been working on were drastically different than the ones he'd seen earlier. He discovered that he'd rounded one of the variables to the thousandth place rather than the millionth as he'd done in all the simulations previously. That miniscule deviation in temperature or wind speed drastically altered the weather predictions for the next two months. He surmised that even the flap of a butterfly wing could determine whether or not a tornado developed in the Midwest.[29]

The power of our impact begins where we are. When we implement these skills within our family and immediate workspace, we can instigate small changes in the world. And while we might think they're too insignificant to make a difference, we need to remember that the ripple we create can continue for millennia. An act as simple as the flap of a butterfly wing has the potential to stop an outburst or boost self-esteem.

While the results of using our soft skills is as unpredictable as the effect of a butterfly's flapping on the weather, when we approach every interaction with love and compassion, we create an environment of openness and collaboration. It's easier to embrace the chaos when we come at it from a place of caring and acceptance. Even when the results aren't what we envision, an outlook of love allows us to experience more of life.

The other option is to be closed off and transactional. In which case we lose the ability to cultivate the skills of adaptability, enthusiasm, acceptance, and more. Without this approach of love, we miss seeing others' perspectives which I believe could lead to a horribly apocalyptic scenario.

In an era where it seems we can't choose the tempo of the song, we can choose the intention and mindset we bring to the dance. Our individual choice to act from a place of love affects groups, nations, and the global collective. A group in its collaborative essence oriented around love and the desire to produce positive change with hope and compassion can solve the crisis facing humanity as well as deal with the complexities of our environment. We need to stay engaged to ensure the trends move in the right direction. The concept of the power of love is true. We need to keep it at the forefront of what we do, whether romantic, familial, between friends, or simply toward all fellow humans.

Embrace Uncertainty

Uncertainty reigns. As much as we plan, each day continues to change the music without warning. And though we know life will be radically different for our children when they become adults, we have no idea what that different will look like.

It's not unrealistic to think we could have the ability to cure the worst of diseases, feed all people, address the climate crisis, and make clean, efficient travel widely accessible. The rapid change we face promises a future we can't fully comprehend. Dancing with chaos means looking at the future through eyes of abundance, of what can be, and using this skillset to create the best world possible. My understanding of abundance includes recognizing technological progress and harnessing the exponential curve rather than allowing it to overwhelm us.

Conversely, we can look at the world from a perspective of scarcity, as if there's not enough to go around. That's what happens to those who have a closed mind and transactional mentality. Embracing the chaos means preparing a good life for our children and grandchildren using the advancements at our disposal while anticipating exponential growth over the decades rather than assuming they will live the same life we have today.

The Toolkit

These eighteen skills categorized into three sets—Rooting, Accelerating, and Navigating—will allow you to ground yourself, accelerate with less effort, and navigate in the midst of the chaos. They combine mindsets and behaviors that facilitate accepting and embracing the dance forced upon us by the state of the world.

They don't have to be mastered in the order presented, all at once, or even all to the same degree. If a few jump out at you, they may be the ones you're already good at or are ready to pursue. You may find some intriguing, and as you improve in one area, you might discover one skill aids your growth in another. I encourage you to reread the chapters on the skills you want to pursue more deliberately or skim them for the essentials.

Armed with these tools, you can maintain a positive outlook and see the world as full of potential and abundance. When you feel overwhelmed, consider these skills and ask yourself which one will move the needle. Use the chapter titles to determine which skill needs the most work at that moment. Then practice the practical tips at the end of each chapter to sharpen your skill set.

We've all spent time with people who do nothing but complain about their problems. As you converse with them, you'll realize, they're missing these tools—they haven't learned to dance. Each step we learn shows us how we can make a bigger impact and achieve success.

As I root myself in hope, courage, focus, relationships, creativity, and practice, I continually develop adaptability, confidence, enthusiasm, mental flexibility, acceptance, and competition so I can accelerate to keep up in this ever-changing, exponentially moving world. Then, by using perseverance, prioritization, pragmatism, collaboration, learning, and the art of slowing down, I can better navigate the restless waters.

More than anything, I want you to experience freedom in the midst of this unprecedented transitional and transformational time. This freedom comes when we embrace these skills, have the courage to change the things in our power to change and accept the tempo of the music. Only then can we truly move with the rhythm of the culture, enjoy the motion of life, and keep up with the speed of exponential change. Only after we embrace the pandemonium can we leave behind the fear of uncertainty and begin Dancing with Chaos.

Endnotes

1   Siegler, MC. Tech Crunch "Eric Schmidt: Every 2 Days We Create as Much Information As We Did up to 2003." https://techcrunch.com/2010/08/04/schmidt-data/

2   Lodestar Solutions. "How Fast is Knowledge Doubling?" Accessed July 19, 2023. https://lodestarsolutions.com/keeping-up-with-the-surge-of-information-and-human-knowledge/

3   Harvard Business Review, Breakthrough Ideas for Tomorrow's Business Agenda April 2003. cited in "Dr. Daniel Goleman Explains the History of Emotional Intelligence" by Joshua Friedman at 6seconds.org January 30, 2005.

4   Katz, Leslie. *CNET.* "How tech and social media are making us feel lonelier than ever." June 18, 2020. https://www.cnet.com/culture/features/how-tech-and-social-media-are-making-us-feel-lonelier-than-ever/

5   Groth, Leah. *Everyday Health.* "9 Reasons Dancing is Good for Your Health." July 6, 2022. https://www.everydayhealth. com/fitness-pictures/health-benefits-of-dance.aspx

6   "3 Inspiring Short Stories about Hope to Power Your Life" *WinnersStory.* July 20, 2022. https://winnersstory.com/short-stories-hope-1.

7   "Our Founder, Father Greg." *Homeboy Industries.* Accessed July 21, 2023. https://homeboyindustries.org/our-story/father-greg/.

8   (Zhou, Luisa. *Luisa Zhou* "The Percentage of Businesses that Fail." March 7, 2023. https://www.luisazhou.com/blog/businesses-that-fail/

9   *Apollo Technical Engineered Talent Solutions.* "17 Remarkable Career Change Statistics to Know." December 4, 2022. https://www.apollotechnical.com/career-change-statistics/.

10 Yesilevich, Allen. *Mastering the Fear of Change.* October 18, 2019. https://www.linkedin.com/pulse/mastering-fear-change-allen-yesilevich.

11 *Free Agent* "New Research Reveals Half of Brits Admit to Being Scared of Change." March 10, 2019. https://www.free-agent.com/us/company/press-room/fear-of-change-research/

12 Sol, Mateo. *Loner Wolf.* "Eternally Connected: How Technology Disconnects You From Yourself." February 18, 2022. https://lonerwolf.com/technology-disconnects/

13 Vitasek, Kate. *Forbes.* "Why Collaboration Yields Improved Productivity (And The Science Behind It)" March 8, 2022 https://www.forbes.com/sites/katevitasek/2022/03/08/why-collaboration-yields-improved-productivity-and-the-science-behind-it/?sh=2ec7966d5d55

14 Novotney, Amy. *American Psychological Association.* "The Risk of Social Isolation." May 2019 https://www.apa.org/monitor/2019/05/ce-corner-isolation

15 Broida, Rick. *CBS News Money Watch*. "How to Remember Names." June 8, 2007. https://www.cbsnews.com/news/how-to-remember-names/

16 *BBC* "Dunbar's number: Why we can only maintain 150 relationships." October 9, 2019. https://www.bbc.com/future/article/20191001-dunbars-number-why-we-can-only-maintain-150-relationships.

17 Cherry, Kendra. *VeryWell Mind* "What is Neuroplasticity?" Updated November 8, 2022. https://www.verywellmind.com/what-is-brain-plasticity-2794886

18 *Better Aging.* "The Importance of Neuroplasticity As We Age." June 1, 2021 https://www.betteraging.com/aging-science/the-importance-of-neuroplasticity-as-we-age/

19 Rosengran, Phil. *BetterPitching.com* "Deliberate Practice: Talent is Overrated. Accessed July 28, 2023. https://betterpitching.com/deliberate-practice-talent-is-overrated/.

20 Bezos, Jeff. *Harvard Business Review*. "How Amazon Thinks About Competition." December 21, 2020. https://hbr.org/2020/12/how-amazon-thinks-about-competition

21 Leonard, Michael. *Inspire Your Success.* "8 Inspiring Perseverance Stories to Make You Never Give Up." Accessed December 23, 2023. https://www.inspireyoursuccess.com/inspiring-perseverance-stories/.

22 Godin, Seth. "Polishing perfect." *Seth's Blog*, June 11, 2013, https://seths.blog/2013/06/polishing-perfect.

23 Oberbrunner, Kary. *The E-mind*. (Ohio: Ethos Collective, 2023).

24 *Wikipedia*. "Wikipedia Statistics." Accessed December 26, 2023. https://en.wikipedia.org/wiki/Wikipedia: Statistics#

25 Raghupathi, Viju & Raghupathi, Wullianallur. *Archives of Public Health.* "The influence of education on health: an empirical assessment of OECD countries for the period 1995–2015." https://archpublichealth.biomedcentral.com/articles/10.1186/s13690-020-00402-5

26 Kaye, Randy and Drash, Wayne. *CNN*. "Kids for Sale: My Mom Was Tricked." October 13, 2017. https://www.cnn.com/2017/10/12/health/uganda-adoptions-investigation-ac360/index.html.

27 Miller, Greg. Smithsonian Magazine. "How Does Breathing Affect Your Brain?" October 18, 2022. https://www.smithsonianmag.com/science-nature/how-does-breathing-affect-your-brain-180980950/

28 *World Vision*. "Global Hunger Facts." Accessed August 28, 2023. https://30hourfamine.worldvision.org/index.cfm?fuseaction=cms.page&id=3852

29 Dizikes, Peter. *MIT Technology Review*. "When the Butterfly Effect Took Flight. February 22, 2011. https://www.technologyreview.com/2011/02/22/196987/when-the-butterfly-effect-took-flight/

Solution to Dot Puzzle from Chapter 5

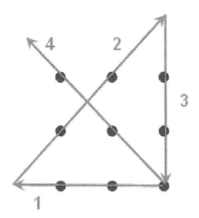

About the Author

From Boston to Paris, Carly Abramowitz has always danced to her own rhythmic beat. A graduate of Northwestern

University, she's not just an innovator, but a dynamic force of creativity and energy in a world of constant change.

Driven by depth, purpose, and an insatiable zest for life, Carly founded CA Consulting Group in 2005. Today, the international firm stands at the forefront of elevating leadership, sales, and communication training for global giants.

Carly's signature learning methodology intertwines rhythmic design and high-energy experiences with a hands-on and practice-based approach. It's not just about learning; it's about transformative experiences that catalyze real change on both the personal and organizational spectrum.

Recently, Carly and her team pioneered a multiplayer digital learning system that reimagines soft skills training. Rooted in storytelling and collective practice, this platform is reshaping how to solidify key Edge Skills™ like adaptability, emotional intelligence, mental flexibility, and assertiveness.

While experiences from institutions like Harvard's Launching New Ventures, Singularity University, and Abundance360, illuminate her expertise, it's Carly's vivacious spirit that truly sets her apart. As a CEO, she champions the imperative of perpetual learning and adaptability in a world that's evolving at breakneck speed. She believes that in our rapid, ever-shifting world, it's our inner growth and depth that will determine our outer success.

Balancing the allure of Paris with the vibrant energy of Miami, Carly, alongside her two children, gracefully navigates between these two worlds.

Connect with Carly at

CONNECT WITH CARLY

Follow her on your favorite social media platforms today.

CAConsulting-Group.com

EMPOWERMENT THROUGH TRANSFORMATIVE COACHING AND TRAINING

Unlock your team's potential to flourish in a world of change with CA Consulting Group

CA CONSULTING GROUP

CAConsulting-Group.com

EXPERIENCE THE DYNAMISM OF CARLY ABRAMOWITZ IN ACTION

Captivating keynotes that weave creativity with practicality for today's evolving challenges.

KEYNOTE SPEAKER

START THE CONVERSATION TODAY

DancingwithChaos.com

TALK WITH GENIE

Discover your individual path to success with Genie - a personal guide offering bespoke, actionable insights for a life in harmony with change.

DancingWithChaos.com/Genie

THIS BOOK IS PROTECTED INTELLECTUAL PROPERTY

Instant IP ™

The author of this book values Intellectual Property. The book you just read is protected by Instant IP™, a proprietary process, which integrates blockchain technology giving Intellectual Property "Global Protection." By creating a "Time-Stamped" smart contract that can never be tampered with or changed, we establish "First Use" that tracks back to the author.

Instant IP™ functions much like a Pre-Patent™ since it provides an immutable "First Use" of the Intellectual Property. This is achieved through our proprietary process of leveraging blockchain technology and smart contracts. As a result, proving "First Use" is simple through a global and verifiable smart contract. By protecting intellectual property with blockchain technology and smart contracts, we establish a "First to File" event.

Protected by Instant IP ™

LEARN MORE AT INSTANTIP.TODAY

Printed by Amazon Italia Logistica S.r.l.
Torrazza Piemonte (TO), Italy

63757733R00152